The Maxtrend System

THE MAXTREND SYSTEM

By Donald S. Mart

Foreword

In 1981, my original "Master Trading Formula" text was published. At that time, only the four major metals that are traded in the futures market (Gold, Silver, Copper, and Platinum) had been developed and thoroughly tested for use with the Formula. Because of the success in trading the four metals futures with the Formula, numerous inquiries and requests were received asking if the Formula could be expanded to include other commodity futures.

Now, over four years later, after literally hundreds of additional hours of computer analysis and market testing, a new formula has been born—one that is not only a vast improvement over the Master Trading Formula, but one that adds another nine commodities to the portfolio, making a total of 13 commodities in all. This new system is called MAXTREND.

Within the pages of this text are the complete formulas, factors, and instructions necessary for you to easily calculate and apply the new Maxtrend System to the commodity futures market. You will also find full historical performance runs for all 13 commodity futures for up to seven years each, suggested trading portfolios ranging from $10,000 to $100,000, and worksheet masters for you to copy and use in your daily calculations.

May you have the very best of trading success when using "The Maxtrend System."

Donald S. Mart

Acknowledgement

Stephan M. Sperling, a perfect blending of commodity futures and computer expert. With a Certificate of Philosophy in mathematics, a reputation as one of the finest computer system analysts and programmers in the country, and a profound knowledge of commodities, commodity markets and commodity trading, no one could have been more suited to perform the computer work necessary to validate and document Maxtrend than Mr. Sperling.

My heartfelt thanks to him for his invaluable contribution to the realization of this book.

Table of Contents

Illustrations

Introduction

"Nothing good comes easy." An old adage that still holds true. In your hands, right now, is the way to make consistent profits trading in futures, but you are going to have to spend some time learning, applying, and then gearing yourself mentally and emotionally to an almost completely automatic way of trading. The last will probably be the most difficult. Forget your own judgment and intuitive feelings, and the market letters you receive, and your broker's advice, and all the "hot" information. The only thing that must concern you is the trading signal that you calculate each day for the next day's trading. Stick with the signal and you have every opportunity to profit; deviate from it, just once, and you have negated the systematic trading that is the key to consistent trading success in the futures market.

The Maxtrend System is based on the premise that in whatever manner fundamental and technical traders, floor brokers, producers and users of the basic products (or major external forces such as government or foreign buyers and sellers) affect the trading action of the market, their actions are always reflected in the price movement—the highs, the lows, the openings, and the closes. As an illustration, the high price of a commodity on a given day is the consensus of optimism (or bullishness) that was available from all factors in the market that day to attain that price; conversely, the low price contains all of the negative factors (or bearishness) available. The closing price, relatively speaking, is the balance point of the trading sentiment for that day. Therefore, the *price movement* becomes a significant and reliable barometer on which to base trading action, and is ideal for analysis and interpretation by a computer.

Early in the computer analysis stage of The Maxtrend System, it was discovered that a relatively long-term, trend-following trading method was one of the more solid approaches to successful futures trading. Starting with that knowledge, Maxtrend was designed to do the following:

1. Provide *exact* buy and sell signals for entering the market and for liquidation.
2. Signal trend movements *soon enough* to take advantage of most of the move.
3. Signal trend reversals *quick enough* to protect profits, without excessive false signals or whipsaws.

13

4. Normally *limit losing trades* to reasonable amounts with effectively placed stop orders.
5. Being basically a long-term trading method, The Maxtrend System greatly reduces commission charges and *allows large gains* when a trend is captured.
6. Being a mechanical trading system, The Maxtrend System *removes* the decision-making quandary from the trader by making each trade *automatic*, thereby helping eliminate emotionalism and judgment error.

As you become more familiar with Maxtrend it will become apparent that the system meets most criteria for capital conservation, profit-making capability, and winning consistency. More important, it now places in your hands a tool of confidence and strength with which to trade profitably and securely in the futures markets.

Chapter One

The System

The Maxtrend System is a trend-following trading method. It never attempts to pick a bottom or top to a market, but rather awaits confirmation of what hopefully will be a major trend, then attempts to capture the "middle" of the move. So as not to miss this major trend, you, the trader, will constantly have a position either *long* or *short* in the market. That is, once you have made your initial entry into the market, you will always be in it, in one direction or the other.

To draw an analogy, Maxtrend is like going fishing. It is constantly seeking (fishing) for a trend in the market (either up or down). When a signal is reached, it is a good indication that the market is taking that direction. If the signal is false and the market reverses, you will most likely absorb a loss by being "stopped-out," but you will also, *at the same moment,* be "stopped-in" to a new position in the opposite direction (reversing). This is like getting nibbles, losing your bait, then putting new bait on your hook. Finally, when the market begins a definite trend, you will "automatically" be in the right position (like getting a solid strike and landing the fish).

THE THEORY OF THE MAXTREND SYSTEM

The Maxtrend System is a complex, linearly weighted, exponentially smoothed moving average system. It is based on assigning the most importance to what has occurred *most recently* in the market, this importance diminishing linearly as new events occur. Volatility of the market, which is determined in a new and innovative fashion, dictates the exponential smoothing, allowing Maxtrend to adjust to violent, swinging markets, or to placid, trending markets, or to any other type of market action at any price level. It is this flexibility to adjust to changing market conditions and price levels that makes Maxtrend a superior tool for trading in futures.

GETTING STARTED

Sharpen your pencil, you are going to need it. It is estimated that once you have become adept in using Maxtrend, it will take you approximately ten minutes each day to hand calculate your trading signal for each future for the next day. If you use a programmable calculator or computer, it should take less than one minute.

The Maxtrend System, with full operating instructions, is available in software form for the IBM-PC or XT (and their compatibles), the TRS-80 (IV), or on magnetic program cards for the handheld Hewlett-Packard HP-41CV or CX. These aids can be obtained from:

Lambert Programming Service
434 N. Crescent Heights Boulevard
Los Angeles, California 90048
(213) 658-6284

As an alternative to you performing all of the work, a fully managed trading account under The Maxtrend System is available from the following futures brokerage firm:

Wilshire Trading Co., Inc.
122 S. Robertson Boulevard
Suite 300
Los Angeles, California 90048
(213) 274-1689

By contacting either of the above, full information will be sent to you regarding their services.

SETTING UP A WORK SHEET AND TRADE RECORD

Setting up a work sheet and trade record to keep track of all of your daily computations, results, trading actions, etc., is an absolute necessity and is quite easy. Just refer to the partially completed sample "Work Sheet & Trade Record" at the back of this text to get an idea of how to record your data and computations. Blank "Work Sheet & Trade Record" forms have also been supplied for your use (remember to save at least one for photocopying for future needs). As you progress through Maxtrend, the meaning and use of each column heading will become apparent.

Note: Before proceeding, keep in mind that the word *"today,"* when used in the text, represents any day *after* the market has closed for that day.

DETERMINING THE DAILY PRICE AVERAGE (DPA)*

The first calculation that we must perform is to obtain the "average" trading action for the day for the futures contract you are trading. (The months you trade will be discussed in a later section). Instead of using just the closing price as the trading criteria for that day, we will take the high, low, and close of the day, add them together and divide that sum by three, which gives us a much more representative model of the day's trading profile.

Example:

July 1980 Copper:

    Date: 8/14/84   High: 91.35

                         Low: 89.60

                         Close: 91.25

                         272.20 ÷ 3 = 90.733 Daily Price Average (DPA)

Note: Throughout the book, whenever calculations or descriptive examples are given, we will use the July 1980 Copper contract trading history as the basis for those examples. Calculations are performed *in the same manner* for all futures, with only the numerical factors used in the calculations being different for each future.

---

* You must learn the few abbreviations that are contained in this book—they are used throughout the text. So that you can refer to these abbreviations and their meanings without having to find individual pages, we have included a Glossary of Abbreviations for your convenience in the back section of this book.

The System

DETERMINING VOLATILITY

The next calculation that you must learn is how to determine the volatility of the futures contract you are trading. Maxtrend uses a blending of two volatility measurements; the first a commonly used measure involving daily ranges, the second a unique measure, often overlooked, yet critical for the true measurement of market volatility when doing a long-term trend-following form of trading.

VOLATILITY MEASUREMENT I:
DETERMINING ACTUAL RANGE VOLATILITY

Volatility, in one form, can be directly related to range (amount of price movement in a given period of time). A simple measurement is shown by the ordinary bar used in bar charts to show the range of a day's trading.

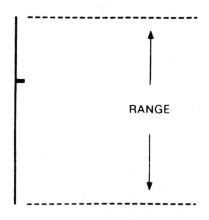

Figure 1
A Single Day's Trading Range

As can be seen in Figure 1, the range is the distance from the lowest point to the highest point of the bar. Now, if you were interested only in day trading (where one enters and exits a trade all in the same day), then the range shown in Figure 1 would be a measurement that could be used almost exclusively. But, for trading where a position is held for more than a day, a refinement has to be made to allow for limit up or limit down trading days (Figure 2), or days when a gap between yesterday's close and the highest or lowest point attained in today's trading makes the range greater than the range (low to high) of just today's trading (Figure 3). We will call this Actual Range.

As can be seen from Figures 1 through 3, Actual Range then is the maximum distance that the price moved, either during today's trading or from yesterday's close to the farthest price point reached today. It follows, then, that Actual Range is the *greatest* one of the following three measurements:

A. The distance from today's low to today's high, or

B. The distance from yesterday's close to today's low, or

C. The distance from yesterday's close to today's high.

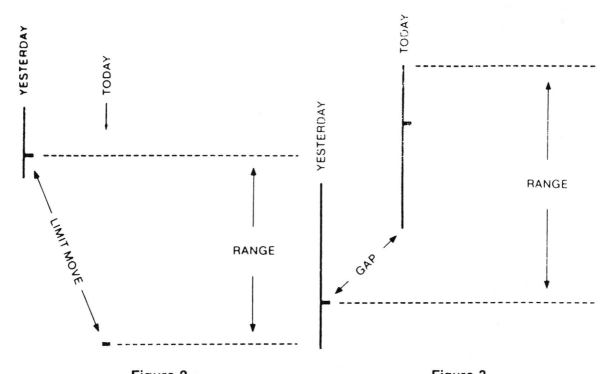

Figure 2
Actual Range for a Limit Movement Day

Figure 3
Actual Range for a Gap Movement Day

One day's range, though, does not a market make, and to be valid as a measurement of volatility, an average of a number of days' ranges must be calculated to arrive at an Average Daily Actual Range (ADAR). For Maxtrend, we utilize the most recent 15 days' Actual Ranges of the futures contract being traded to acquire the ADAR.

The System

We already know how to obtain the Actual Range for one day by using the greatest of three ranges (A, B, or C) shown in Figure 4. We shall call this Actual Range for one day, ARO (Actual Range One).

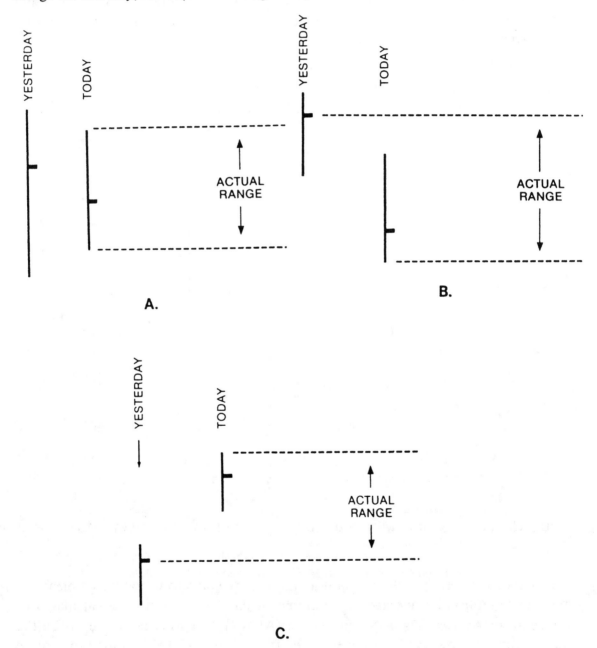

Figure 4
Actual Range Determination

20

To arrive at the ADAR *initially,* add the ARO's for the past 15 days and divide by 15. This figure is used as the Previous Average Daily Actual Range (PADAR) in the following equation which will be used to obtain all subsequent ADAR's. This equation levels out large short-term jumps in the ADAR by exponentially smoothing it, and also allows having to maintain data only for the previous day instead of for a 15-day period.

The equation for obtaining the exponentially smoothed ADAR is:

Average Daily Actual Range (ADAR) =

$$\frac{14 \times \text{Previous Average Daily Actual Range (PADAR)} + \text{Today's Actual Range (ARO)}}{15}$$

The following table is an actual example utilizing the July 1980 Copper contract on how to obtain the ADAR on a daily basis:

Example Of Obtaining The Average Daily Actual Range (ADAR)
July 1980 COPPER

Day	Date	High	Low	Close	ARO Measurement	ARO	ADAR
	8/01/79	—	—	85.65	—	—	
1	8/02/79	87.00	85.30	87.00	low to high	1.70	
2	8/03/79	87.70	86.00	86.00	low to high	1.70	
3	8/06/79	86.35	84.80	86.35	low to high	1.55	
4	8/07/79	87.25	86.70	86.70	prev. close to high	.90	
5	8/08/79	88.05	87.10	88.05	prev. close to high	1.35	
6	8/09/79	89.30	87.40	89.30	low to high	1.90	
7	8/10/79	89.50	88.70	89.15	low to high	.80	
8	8/13/79	88.75	87.90	88.35	prev. close to low	1.25	
9	8/14/79	91.35	89.60	91.25	prev. close to high	3.00	
10	8/15/79	91.40	90.50	90.65	low to high	.90	
11	8/16/79	90.75	89.65	89.85	low to high	1.10	
12	8/17/79	90.30	89.65	89.90	low to high	.65	
13	8/20/79	90.30	88.25	88.25	low to high	2.05	
14	8/21/79	90.00	88.55	90.00	prev. close to high	1.75	
15	8/22/79	90.50	88.60	88.60	low to high	1.90	1.50
16	8/23/79	90.50	88.65	90.25	prev. close to high	1.90	1.53
17	8/24/79	92.30	91.10	91.85	prev. close to high	2.05	1.56
18	and on...						

The System

Starting off, we add the ARO's for the first 15 days shown above and obtain a total of 22.5, which we divide by 15 to obtain our first ADAR, which is 1.50 for 8/22/79.

From this point on, we use the previously stated equation to determine our ADAR:

$$ADAR = \frac{14 \times PADAR + ARO}{15}$$

Following is how you would determine the ADAR for 8/23/79:

$$\frac{14 \times 1.50 \text{ (the previous days ADAR)} + 1.90 \text{ (today's ARO)}}{15} =$$

$$\frac{21 + 1.90}{15} =$$

$$\frac{22.9}{15} = 1.526 \text{ (round off)} = 1.53 \text{ (the new ADAR for 8/23/79)}.$$

As one further example to make sure you understand the process, let us determine the ADAR for 8/24/79:

$$\frac{14 \times 1.53 \text{ (the 8/23/79 ADAR)} + 2.05 \text{ (today's ARO)}}{15} =$$

$$\frac{21.42 + 2.05}{15} =$$

$$\frac{23.47}{15} = 1.564 \text{ (round off)} = 1.56 \text{ (the new ADAR for 8/24/79)}.$$

Briefly, in review, here are the rules for obtaining your daily ADAR:

1. Add the first 15 days' ARO's together and divide by 15; this will give you the ADAR for the 15th day.

2. Thereafter, use the ADAR for the previous day (the PADAR), multiply it by 14, add the ARO for today and divide this sum by 15. That's all there is to it.

Now that we have obtained our ADAR, we must quantify it as a factor of volatility. This factor will be called the Actual Range Volatility Factor (ARVF). Simply take the ADAR and locate it in the appropriate futures table that follows (they are listed in alphabetical order). As an example, take the first ADAR we calculated for July 1980 Copper from the previous table (an ADAR of 1.50) and locate it in the ADAR column of the Copper Actual Range Volatility table. As you can see, there are 21 ARVF "grades," increasing in size with increased volatility. Our example number of 1.50 falls in the 1.35 to 1.58 range, giving the copper an ARVF of 7 for the next market day. The ARVF is used along with the second volatility factor to determine our final volatility factor.

COFFEE ACTUAL RANGE VOLATILITY
(Volatility Measurement I)

If Average Daily Actual Range (ADAR) is		The Actual Range Volatility Factor (ARVF) is
Over	But Not Over	
Pts.	Pts.	
0.00	0.18	1
0.18	0.36	2
0.36	0.54	3
0.54	0.72	4
0.72	0.90	5
0.90	1.08	6
1.08	1.26	7
1.26	1.44	8
1.44	1.62	9
1.62	1.80	10
1.80	1.98	11
1.98	2.16	12
2.16	2.34	13
2.34	2.52	14
2.52	2.70	15
2.70	2.88	16
2.88	3.06	17
3.06	3.24	18
3.24	3.42	19
3.42	3.60	20
3.60	—	21

COPPER ACTUAL RANGE VOLATILITY
(Volatility Measurement I)

**If Average Daily
Actual Range (ADAR) is**

Over	But Not Over	The Actual Range Volatility Factor (ARVF) is
Pts.	Pts.	
0.00	0.23	1
0.23	0.45	2
0.45	0.68	3
0.68	0.90	4
0.90	1.13	5
1.13	1.35	6
1.35	1.58	7
1.58	1.80	8
1.80	2.03	9
2.03	2.25	10
2.25	2.48	11
2.48	2.70	12
2.70	2.93	13
2.93	3.15	14
3.15	3.38	15
3.38	3.60	16
3.60	3.83	17
3.83	4.05	18
4.05	4.28	19
4.28	4.50	20
4.50	—	21

GOLD ACTUAL RANGE VOLATILITY
(Volatility Measurement I)

**If Average Daily
Actual Range (ADAR) is**

Over	But Not Over	The Actual Range Volatility Factor (ARVF) is
US$	US$	
0.00	1.13	1
1.13	2.25	2
2.25	3.38	3
3.38	4.50	4
4.50	5.63	5
5.63	6.75	6
6.75	7.88	7
7.88	9.00	8
9.00	10.13	9
10.13	11.25	10
11.25	12.38	11
12.38	13.50	12
13.50	14.63	13
14.63	15.75	14
15.75	16.88	15
16.88	18.00	16
18.00	19.13	17
19.13	20.25	18
20.25	21.38	19
21.38	22.50	20
22.50	—	21

HEATING OIL NO. 2 ACTUAL RANGE VOLATILITY
(Volatility Measurement I)

**If Average Daily
Actual Range (ADAR) is**

Over	But Not Over	The Actual Range Volatility Factor (ARVF) is
Pts.	Pts.	
0.00	0.09	1
0.09	0.18	2
0.18	0.27	3
0.27	0.36	4
0.36	0.45	5
0.45	0.54	6
0.54	0.63	7
0.63	0.72	8
0.72	0.81	9
0.81	0.90	10
0.90	0.99	11
0.99	1.08	12
1.08	1.17	13
1.17	1.26	14
1.26	1.35	15
1.35	1.44	16
1.44	1.53	17
1.53	1.62	18
1.62	1.71	19
1.71	1.80	20
1.80	—	21

JAPANESE YEN ACTUAL RANGE VOLATILITY
(Volatility Measurement I)

**If Average Daily
Actual Range (ADAR) is**

Over	But Not Over	The Actual Range Volatility Factor (ARVF) is
Pts.	Pts.	
0.0000	0.0004	1
0.0004	0.0008	2
0.0008	0.0012	3
0.0012	0.0016	4
0.0016	0.0020	5
0.0020	0.0024	6
0.0024	0.0028	7
0.0028	0.0032	8
0.0032	0.0036	9
0.0036	0.0040	10
0.0040	0.0044	11
0.0044	0.0048	12
0.0048	0.0052	13
0.0052	0.0056	14
0.0056	0.0060	15
0.0060	0.0064	16
0.0064	0.0068	17
0.0068	0.0072	18
0.0072	0.0076	19
0.0076	0.0080	20
0.0080	—	21

NYSE COMPOSITE ACTUAL RANGE VOLATILITY
(Volatility Measurement I)

If Average Daily
Actual Range (ADAR) is

Over	But Not Over	The Actual Range Volatility Factor (ARVF) is
Pts.	Pts.	
0.00	0.15	1
0.15	0.30	2
0.30	0.45	3
0.45	0.60	4
0.60	0.75	5
0.75	0.90	6
0.90	1.05	7
1.05	1.20	8
1.20	1.35	9
1.35	1.50	10
1.50	1.65	11
1.65	1.80	12
1.80	1.95	13
1.95	2.10	14
2.10	2.25	15
2.25	2.40	16
2.40	2.55	17
2.55	2.70	18
2.70	2.85	19
2.85	3.00	20
3.00	—	21

PLATINUM ACTUAL RANGE VOLATILITY
(Volatility Measurement I)

If Average Daily
Actual Range (ADAR) is

Over	But Not Over	The Actual Range Volatility Factor (ARVF) is
US$	US$	
0.00	0.90	1
0.90	1.80	2
1.80	2.70	3
2.70	3.60	4
3.60	4.50	5
4.50	5.40	6
5.40	6.30	7
6.30	7.20	8
7.20	8.10	9
8.10	9.00	10
9.00	9.90	11
9.90	10.80	12
10.80	11.70	13
11.70	12.60	14
12.60	13.50	15
13.50	14.40	16
14.40	15.30	17
15.30	16.20	18
16.20	17.10	19
17.10	18.00	20
18.00	—	21

PORK BELLIES ACTUAL RANGE VOLATILITY
(Volatility Measurement I)

If Average Daily
Actual Range (ADAR) is

Over	But Not Over	The Actual Range Volatility Factor (ARVF) is
Pts.	Pts.	
0.00	0.09	1
0.09	0.18	2
0.18	0.27	3
0.27	0.36	4
0.36	0.45	5
0.45	0.54	6
0.54	0.63	7
0.63	0.72	8
0.72	0.81	9
0.81	0.90	10
0.90	0.99	11
0.99	1.08	12
1.08	1.17	13
1.17	1.26	14
1.26	1.35	15
1.35	1.44	16
1.44	1.53	17
1.53	1.62	18
1.62	1.71	19
1.71	1.80	20
1.80	—	21

SILVER ACTUAL RANGE VOLATILITY
(Volatility Measurement I)

If Average Daily
Actual Range (ADAR) is

Over	But Not Over	The Actual Range Volatility Factor (ARVF) is
US¢	US¢	
0.00	2.25	1
2.25	4.50	2
4.50	6.75	3
6.75	9.00	4
9.00	11.25	5
11.25	13.50	6
13.50	15.75	7
15.75	18.00	8
18.00	20.25	9
20.25	22.50	10
22.50	24.75	11
24.75	27.00	12
27.00	29.25	13
29.25	31.50	14
31.50	33.75	15
33.75	36.00	16
36.00	38.25	17
38.25	40.50	18
40.50	42.75	19
42.75	45.00	20
45.00	—	21

SOYBEANS* ACTUAL RANGE VOLATILITY
(Volatility Measurement I)

If Average Daily
Actual Range (ADAR) is

Over	But Not Over	The Actual Range Volatility Factor (ARVF) is
US¢	US¢	
0.00	1.35	1
1.35	2.70	2
2.70	4.05	3
4.05	5.40	4
5.40	6.75	5
6.75	8.10	6
8.10	9.45	7
9.45	10.80	8
10.80	12.15	9
12.15	13.50	10
13.50	14.85	11
14.85	16.20	12
16.20	17.55	13
17.55	18.90	14
18.90	20.25	15
20.25	21.60	16
21.60	22.95	17
22.95	24.30	18
24.30	25.65	19
25.65	27.00	20
27.00	—	21

* Soybean prices are quoted in fractions of cents, rather than in decimals, but for purposes of computation, these fractions are converted into decimals.

SOYBEAN MEAL ACTUAL RANGE VOLATILITY
(Volatility Measurement I)

If Average Daily
Actual Range (ADAR) is

Over	But Not Over	The Actual Range Volatility Factor (ARVF) is
US$	US$	
0.00	0.45	1
0.45	0.90	2
0.90	1.35	3
1.35	1.80	4
1.80	2.25	5
2.25	2.70	6
2.70	3.15	7
3.15	3.60	8
3.60	4.05	9
4.05	4.50	10
4.50	4.95	11
4.95	5.40	12
5.40	5.85	13
5.85	6.30	14
6.30	6.75	15
6.75	7.20	16
7.20	7.65	17
7.65	8.10	18
8.10	8.55	19
8.55	9.00	20
9.00	—	21

SUGAR (WORLD) ACTUAL RANGE VOLATILITY
(Volatility Measurement I)

If Average Daily
Actual Range (ADAR) is

Over	But Not Over	The Actual Range Volatility Factor (ARVF) is
Pts.	Pts.	
0.00	0.02	1
0.02	0.05	2
0.05	0.07	3
0.07	0.09	4
0.09	0.11	5
0.11	0.14	6
0.14	0.16	7
0.16	0.18	8
0.18	0.20	9
0.20	0.23	10
0.23	0.25	11
0.25	0.27	12
0.27	0.29	13
0.29	0.32	14
0.32	0.34	15
0.34	0.36	16
0.36	0.38	17
0.38	0.41	18
0.41	0.43	19
0.43	0.45	20
0.45	—	21

TREASURY BILLS ACTUAL RANGE VOLATILITY
(Volatility Measurement I)

If Average Daily
Actual Range (ADAR) is

Over	But Not Over	The Actual Range Volatility Factor (ARVF) is
Pts.	Pts.	
0.00	0.03	1
0.03	0.05	2
0.05	0.08	3
0.08	0.11	4
0.11	0.14	5
0.14	0.16	6
0.16	0.19	7
0.19	0.22	8
0.22	0.24	9
0.24	0.27	10
0.27	0.30	11
0.30	0.32	12
0.32	0.35	13
0.35	0.38	14
0.38	0.41	15
0.41	0.43	16
0.43	0.46	17
0.46	0.49	18
0.49	0.51	19
0.51	0.54	20
0.54	—	21

The System

VOLATILITY MEASUREMENT II: DETERMINING PRICE DIFFERENTIAL VOLATILITY

The second measure of volatility is simple to calculate, but the logic of the theory behind its use is critical to judging actual volatility. If you will think for a moment about our first measurement, you will remember that it determines the volatility of daily ranges, but not of direction or momentum. For all of its important value, the first measurement could be in a market going straight sideways with no trend at all, just high volatility days in a tight range. But, this second volatility measurement not only determines a broader range, it gives an indication of directional movement and of momentum. Combined with the first, these two measurements together form an advance-in-the-state-of-the-art criteria for determining true volatility.

To determine Price Differential Range (PDR), simply subtract the *lowest low* from the *highest high* of the *latest* 15 trading days.

Example:

July 1980 Copper:

Date: 8/15/79 Highest High of Initial 15-Day Period:	91.40
8/06/79 Lowest Low of Initial 15-Day Period:	− 84.80
Price Differential Range (PDR):	6.60

Note: You must use only the current 15 days to obtain the highest high and the lowest low when calculating the PDR. Therefore, you must always include today's high and low and drop off the oldest day's (now the 16th day back) high and low each day.

Now that we have obtained our PDR, we must quantify it as a factor of volatility, as we did the ADAR in our first measurement of volatility. This factor will be called the Price Differential Volatility Factor (PDVF). Take the PDR and locate it in the appropriate futures table that follows. As an example, take the PDR we have previously calculated for July 1980 Copper (a PDR of 6.60) and locate it in the PDR column of the Copper Price Differential Volatility table. There are 21 PDVF "grades," increasing in size with increased volatility. Our example number of 6.60 falls in the 5.25 to 7.00 range, giving the copper a PDVF of 4 for the next market day. The PDVF is used along with the first volatility factor to determine our final volatility factor, the Correlated Volatility Factor (CVF).

30

COFFEE PRICE DIFFERENTIAL VOLATILITY
(Volatility Measurement II)

If Price Differential Range (PDR) is

Over	But Not Over	The Price Differential Volatility Factor (PDVF) is
Pts.	Pts.	
0.00	1.40	1
1.40	2.80	2
2.80	4.20	3
4.20	5.60	4
5.60	7.00	5
7.00	8.40	6
8.40	9.80	7
9.80	11.20	8
11.20	12.60	9
12.60	14.00	10
14.00	15.40	11
15.40	16.80	12
16.80	18.20	13
18.20	19.60	14
19.60	21.00	15
21.00	22.40	16
22.40	23.80	17
23.80	25.20	18
25.20	26.60	19
26.60	28.00	20
28.00	—	21

COPPER PRICE DIFFERENTIAL VOLATILITY
(Volatility Measurement II)

If Price Differential Range (PDR) is

Over	But Not Over	The Price Differential Volatility Factor (PDVF) is
Pts.	Pts.	
0.00	1.75	1
1.75	3.50	2
3.50	5.25	3
5.25	7.00	4
7.00	8.75	5
8.75	10.50	6
10.50	12.25	7
12.25	14.00	8
14.00	15.75	9
15.75	17.50	10
17.50	19.25	11
19.25	21.00	12
21.00	22.75	13
22.75	24.50	14
24.50	26.25	15
26.25	28.00	16
28.00	29.75	17
29.75	31.50	18
31.50	33.25	19
33.25	35.00	20
35.00	—	21

GOLD PRICE DIFFERENTIAL VOLATILITY
(Volatility Measurement II)

If Price Differential
Range (PDR) is

Over	But Not Over	The Price Differential Volatility Factor (PDVF) is
US$	US$	
0.00	8.80	1
8.80	17.50	2
17.50	26.30	3
26.30	35.00	4
35.00	43.80	5
43.80	52.50	6
52.50	61.30	7
61.30	70.00	8
70.00	78.80	9
78.80	87.50	10
87.50	96.30	11
96.30	105.00	12
105.00	113.80	13
113.80	122.50	14
122.50	131.30	15
131.30	140.00	16
140.00	148.80	17
148.80	157.50	18
157.50	166.30	19
166.30	175.00	20
175.00	—	21

HEATING OIL NO. 2 PRICE DIFFERENTIAL VOLATILITY
(Volatility Measurement II)

If Price Differential
Range (PDR) is

Over	But Not Over	The Price Differential Volatility Factor (PDVF) is
Pts.	Pts.	
0.00	0.70	1
0.70	1.40	2
1.40	2.10	3
2.10	2.80	4
2.80	3.50	5
3.50	4.20	6
4.20	4.90	7
4.90	5.60	8
5.60	6.30	9
6.30	7.00	10
7.00	7.70	11
7.70	8.40	12
8.40	9.10	13
9.10	9.80	14
9.80	10.50	15
10.50	11.20	16
11.20	11.90	17
11.90	12.60	18
12.60	13.30	19
13.30	14.00	20
14.00	—	21

JAPANESE YEN PRICE DIFFERENTIAL VOLATILITY
(Volatility Measurement II)

If Price Differential Range (PDR) is

Over	But Not Over	The Price Differential Volatility Factor (PDVF) is
Pts.	Pts.	
0.0000	0.0035	1
0.0035	0.0070	2
0.0070	0.0105	3
0.0105	0.0140	4
0.0140	0.0175	5
0.0175	0.0210	6
0.0210	0.0245	7
0.0245	0.0280	8
0.0280	0.0315	9
0.0315	0.0350	10
0.0350	0.0385	11
0.0385	0.0420	12
0.0420	0.0455	13
0.0455	0.0490	14
0.0490	0.0525	15
0.0525	0.0560	16
0.0560	0.0595	17
0.0595	0.0630	18
0.0630	0.0665	19
0.0665	0.0700	20
0.0700	—	21

NYSE COMPOSITE PRICE DIFFERENTIAL VOLATILITY
(Volatility Measurement II)

If Price Differential Range (PDR) is

Over	But Not Over	The Price Differential Volatility Factor (PDVF) is
Pts.	Pts.	
0.00	1.05	1
1.05	2.10	2
2.10	3.15	3
3.15	4.20	4
4.20	5.25	5
5.25	6.30	6
6.30	7.35	7
7.35	8.40	8
8.40	9.45	9
9.45	10.50	10
10.50	11.55	11
11.55	12.60	12
12.60	13.65	13
13.65	14.70	14
14.70	15.75	15
15.75	16.80	16
16.80	17.85	17
17.85	18.90	18
18.90	19.95	19
19.95	21.00	20
21.00	—	21

PLATINUM PRICE DIFFERENTIAL VOLATILITY
(Volatility Measurement II)

**If Price Differential
Range (PDR) is**

Over	But Not Over	The Price Differential Volatility Factor (PDVF) is
US$	US$	
0.00	7.00	1
7.00	14.00	2
14.00	21.00	3
21.00	28.00	4
28.00	35.00	5
35.00	42.00	6
42.00	49.00	7
49.00	56.00	8
56.00	63.00	9
63.00	70.00	10
70.00	77.00	11
77.00	84.00	12
84.00	91.00	13
91.00	98.00	14
98.00	105.00	15
105.00	112.00	16
112.00	119.00	17
119.00	126.00	18
126.00	133.00	19
133.00	140.00	20
140.00	—	21

PORK BELLIES PRICE DIFFERENTIAL VOLATILITY
(Volatility Measurement II)

**If Price Differential
Range (PDR) is**

Over	But Not Over	The Price Differential Volatility Factor (PDVF) is
Pts.	Pts.	
0.00	0.70	1
0.70	1.40	2
1.40	2.10	3
2.10	2.80	4
2.80	3.50	5
3.50	4.20	6
4.20	4.90	7
4.90	5.60	8
5.60	6.30	9
6.30	7.00	10
7.00	7.70	11
7.70	8.40	12
8.40	9.10	13
9.10	9.80	14
9.80	10.50	15
10.50	11.20	16
11.20	11.90	17
11.90	12.60	18
12.60	13.30	19
13.30	14.00	20
14.00	—	21

SILVER PRICE DIFFERENTIAL VOLATILITY
(Volatility Measurement II)

If Price Differential
Range (PDR) is

Over	But Not Over	The Price Differential Volatility Factor (PDVF) is
US¢	US¢	
0.00	17.50	1
17.50	35.00	2
35.00	52.50	3
52.50	70.00	4
70.00	87.50	5
87.50	105.00	6
105.00	122.50	7
122.50	140.00	8
140.00	157.50	9
157.50	175.00	10
175.00	192.50	11
192.50	210.00	12
210.00	227.50	13
227.50	245.00	14
245.00	262.50	15
262.50	280.00	16
280.00	297.50	17
297.50	315.00	18
315.00	332.50	19
332.50	350.00	20
350.00	—	21

SOYBEANS* PRICE DIFFERENTIAL VOLATILITY
(Volatility Measurement II)

If Price Differential
Range (PDR) is

Over	But Not Over	The Price Differential Volatility Factor (PDVF) is
US¢	US¢	
0.00	10.50	1
10.50	21.00	2
21.00	31.50	3
31.50	42.00	4
42.00	52.50	5
52.50	63.00	6
63.00	73.50	7
73.50	84.00	8
84.00	94.50	9
94.50	105.00	10
105.00	115.50	11
115.50	126.00	12
126.00	136.50	13
136.50	147.00	14
147.00	157.50	15
157.50	168.00	16
168.00	178.50	17
178.50	189.00	18
189.00	199.50	19
199.50	210.00	20
210.00	—	21

* Soybean prices are quoted in fractions of cents, rather than in decimals, but for purposes of computation, these fractions are converted into decimals.

SOYBEAN MEAL PRICE DIFFERENTIAL VOLATILITY
(Volatility Measurement II)

If Price Differential Range (PDR) is

Over	But Not Over	The Price Differential Volatility Factor (PDVF) is
US$	US$	
0.00	3.50	1
3.50	7.00	2
7.00	10.50	3
10.50	14.00	4
14.00	17.50	5
17.50	21.00	6
21.00	24.50	7
24.50	28.00	8
28.00	31.50	9
31.50	35.00	10
35.00	38.50	11
38.50	42.00	12
42.00	45.50	13
45.50	49.00	14
49.00	52.50	15
52.50	56.00	16
56.00	59.50	17
59.50	63.00	18
63.00	66.50	19
66.50	70.00	20
70.00	—	21

SUGAR (WORLD) PRICE DIFFERENTIAL VOLATILITY
(Volatility Measurement II)

If Price Differential Range (PDR) is

Over	But Not Over	The Price Differential Volatility Factor (PDVF) is
Pts.	Pts.	
0.00	0.18	1
0.18	0.35	2
0.35	0.53	3
0.53	0.70	4
0.70	0.88	5
0.88	1.05	6
1.05	1.23	7
1.23	1.40	8
1.40	1.58	9
1.58	1.75	10
1.75	1.93	11
1.93	2.10	12
2.10	2.28	13
2.28	2.45	14
2.45	2.63	15
2.63	2.80	16
2.80	2.98	17
2.98	3.15	18
3.15	3.33	19
3.33	3.50	20
3.50	—	21

TREASURY BILLS PRICE DIFFERENTIAL VOLATILITY
(Volatility Measurement II)

**If Price Differential
Range (PDR) is**

Over	But Not Over	The Price Differential Volatility Factor (PDVF) is
Pts.	Pts.	
0.00	0.21	1
0.21	0.42	2
0.42	0.63	3
0.63	0.84	4
0.84	1.05	5
1.05	1.26	6
1.26	1.47	7
1.47	1.68	8
1.68	1.89	9
1.89	2.10	10
2.10	2.31	11
2.31	2.52	12
2.52	2.73	13
2.73	2.94	14
2.94	3.15	15
3.15	3.36	16
3.36	3.57	17
3.57	3.78	18
3.78	3.99	19
3.99	4.20	20
4.20	—	21

DETERMINING THE CORRELATED VOLATILITY FACTOR (CVF)

The CVF is a straightforward blending of the two previously determined volatility factors by simple linear weighting. Just add the two factors together, divide by two, and you have the CVF.

Example:

July 1980 Copper:
    ARVF for 8/22/79:   7
    PDVF for 8/22/79:   4
                Total: $11 \div 2 = 5\frac{1}{2}$ (always round up) = 6 (CVF for 8/22/79)

The System

The CVF is the end result of all of the volatility determinations and is used extensively in further calculations for obtaining our final trading signal.

DETERMINING THE CONSTANT FACTOR (CF)

The first use that the Correlated Volatility Factor (CVF) is put to is in determining the Constant Factor (CF) used in the formula for finding the Trend Indicator (TI) of the futures contract being traded. The CF is used to exponentially smooth the TI to conform to current market and price conditions.

To find the required CF, take the CVF for the day and locate it in the following Constant Factors table. Opposite the CVF, in the table, will be a CF value. As an example, using the July 1980 Copper CVF of 6 for 8/22/79, locate it in the CVF column and opposite it you will find a CF of .105. This number will then be used in the TI formula.

Note: The CF's listed in the Constant Factors table are common to all of the futures.

CONSTANT FACTORS

Correlated Volatility Factor (CVF)	Constant Factor (CF)
1	.084
2	.088
3	.092
4	.096
5	.100
6	.105
7	.110
8	.115
9	.120
10	.130
11	.140
12	.150
13	.160
14	.175
15	.190
16	.205
17	.220
18	.240
19	.265
20	.295
21	.330

DETERMINING THE TREND INDICATOR (TI)

There has to be a first day for everything, and so it is with calculating the TI. The first calculation day is unique in that it has no previous TI on which to apply the equation that is used to obtain all subsequent TI's.

To obtain the TI *initially* requires *averaging* the closing price *only* of the last 15 days (the same 15 days used to determine the ADAR and the PDR), but in a special way. We must weight the 15 days in simple linear fashion as follows:

Multiply today's closing price by 15
Multiply the 2nd last day's closing price by 14
Multiply the 3rd last day's closing price by 13
Multiply the 4th last day's closing price by 12
Etc., for the remaining days.

Add the products together and divide by 120 (the total of multipliers used) to obtain the TI for the first day of trading. This figure is used as TI_1 in the following equation that will be used to obtain all subsequent TI's.

Finally, putting all of our previous calculations together, the equation for obtaining the TI is:

$$TI_2 = TI_1 + CF(DPA - TI_1), \text{ where:}$$

TI_1 is the Trend Indicator (TI) that was used for today (calculated yesterday).
CF is the Constant Factor (CF) for use tomorrow (calculated today).
DPA is the Daily Price Average (DPA) for use today (calculated yesterday).
TI_2 is tomorrow's Trend Indicator (TI).

The following table is an actual example utilizing the July 1980 Copper contract on how to obtain the TI on a daily basis.

EXAMPLE OF OBTAINING THE TREND INDICATOR (TI)
July 1980 COPPER

Day	Date	Close	x	Weighting	=	Product	TI
1	8/02/79	87.00		1		87.00	
2	8/03/79	86.00		2		172.00	
3	8/06/79	86.35		3		259.05	
4	8/07/79	86.70		4		346.80	
5	8/08/79	88.05		5		440.25	
6	8/09/79	89.30		6		535.80	
7	8/10/79	89.15		7		624.05	
8	8/13/79	88.35		8		706.80	
9	8/14/79	91.25		9		821.25	
10	8/15/79	90.65		10		906.50	
11	8/16/79	89.85		11		988.35	
12	8/17/79	89.90		12		1078.80	
13	8/20/79	88.25		13		1147.25	
14	8/21/79	90.00		14		1260.00	
15	8/22/79	88.60		15		1329.00	89.19

Starting off, we add the products for the first 15 days shown in the foregoing table and obtain a total of 10,702.90, which we divide by 120 to obtain our first TI, which is 89.190833; rounded off to two decimal places, becomes 89.19 for 8/22/79 (to be used for trading on 8/23/79).

From this point on, we use the previously stated equation to determine our TI.

Following is how you would determine the TI for 8/23/79:

$$TI_2 = TI_1 + CF \quad (DPA - TI_1)$$

$$89.19^* + .105^{**} \quad (89.23^{***} - 89.19^*) = 89.19^{****}$$

Taking the parenthetical ( ) portion of the formula first, we subtract 89.19 (TI$_1$) from 89.23 (DPA), leaving us a remainder of .04, which is then multiplied by .105 (CF), giving us .0042, which, when added to 89.19 (TI$_1$) to obtain TI$_2$, does not have enough significance to change the TI. Therefore, the TI for 8/23/79 remains at 89.19 (to be used for trading on 8/24/79).

When subtracting TI$_1$ from DPA in the parenthetical portion of the formula, very often you will end up with a *negative* number if TI$_1$ is greater than DPA. For example, if the DPA in the formula was hypothetically 89.05 and the TI$_1$ was 89.56, the remainder would be − .51. Multiplying the negative number by the CF will still leave a negative

* The TI for 8/22/79.
** The CF for a CVF of 6.
*** The DPA for 8/22/79.
**** The TI for 8/23/79.

number, therefore, when adding the negative number to TI_1 to obtain TI_2 in the final step of the formula, you will in actuality be subtracting that number.

To make sure that you completely understand how to utilize the formula, we will now compute the TI for 8/24/79:

$$TI_2 = \underline{TI_1} \quad + \quad \underline{CF} \quad (\quad \underline{DPA} \quad - \quad \underline{TI_1} \ )$$
$$89.19† \ + \ .105†† \ (\ 89.80††† \ - \ 89.19† \ ) \ = \ 89.25††††$$

Taking the parenthetical portion of the formula first, we subtract 89.19 from 89.80, leaving us a remainder of .61, which is then multiplied by .105, giving us .0641, which is then added to 89.19, giving us 89.2541 (round off to 89.25), our TI (to be used for trading on 8/27/79).

Note: The TI is not the trading signal, it is the trend indicator. One more calculation is still required to obtain the actual trading number.

DETERMINING THE MASTER TRADING NUMBER (MTN)

We now come to the final calculation, obtaining our *actual trading signal,* which we will call the Master Trading Number (MTN).

The MTN is simply a price above or below (depending on one's position in the market) the TI and is determined by the volatility of the futures contract being traded.

In essence, the MTN creates a trading buffer zone, or envelope, around the TI to reduce excessive whipsaws and to confirm that a possible trend is starting in that direction.

We again use our CVF number, this time to determine an Envelope Factor (EF) that must be added to or subtracted from the TI to give us the MTN. To find the required EF, simply take the CVF for the day and locate it in the appropriate futures table that follows. As an example, using the July 1980 Copper CVF of 6 for 8/22/79, locate it in the CVF column of the Copper Envelope Factors table, and opposite it you will find an EF of 4.65.

---

† The TI for 8/23/79.
†† The CF for a CVF of 6.
††† The DPA for 8/23/79.
†††† The TI for 8/24/79.

COFFEE ENVELOPE FACTORS

If Correlated Volatility Factor (CVF) is	The Envelope Factor (EF) is
	Pts.
1	2.87
2	3.02
3	3.18
4	3.34
5	3.52
6	3.71
7	3.90
8	4.11
9	4.32
10	4.55
11	4.79
12	5.04
13	5.31
14	5.59
15	5.88
16	6.19
17	6.52
18	6.86
19	7.22
20	7.60
21	8.00

COPPER ENVELOPE FACTORS

If Correlated Volatility Factor (CVF) is	The Envelope Factor (EF) is
	Pts.
1	3.55
2	3.75
3	3.95
4	4.15
5	4.40
6	4.65
7	4.90
8	5.15
9	5.40
10	5.70
11	6.00
12	6.30
13	6.65
14	7.00
15	7.35
16	7.75
17	8.15
18	8.55
19	9.00
20	9.50
21	10.00

GOLD ENVELOPE FACTORS

If Correlated Volatility Factor (CVF) is	The Envelope Factor (EF) is
	US$
1	17.90
2	18.90
3	19.90
4	20.90
5	22.00
6	23.20
7	24.40
8	25.70
9	27.00
10	28.40
11	29.90
12	31.50
13	33.20
14	34.90
15	36.80
16	38.70
17	40.70
18	42.90
19	45.10
20	47.50
21	50.00

HEATING OIL NO. 2 ENVELOPE FACTORS

If Correlated Volatility Factor (CVF) is	The Envelope Factor (EF) is
	Pts.
1	1.42
2	1.50
3	1.57
4	1.65
5	1.75
6	1.85
7	1.95
8	2.05
9	2.15
10	2.27
11	2.40
12	2.52
13	2.65
14	2.80
15	2.95
16	3.10
17	3.25
18	3.42
19	3.60
20	3.80
21	4.00

JAPANESE YEN ENVELOPE FACTORS

If Correlated Volatility Factor (CVF) is	The Envelope Factor (EF) is
	Pts.
1	0.0066
2	0.0070
3	0.0074
4	0.0078
5	0.0083
6	0.0088
7	0.0093
8	0.0098
9	0.0104
10	0.0110
11	0.0116
12	0.0123
13	0.0130
14	0.0137
15	0.0145
16	0.0153
17	0.0162
18	0.0171
19	0.0180
20	0.0190
21	0.0200

NYSE COMPOSITE ENVELOPE FACTORS

If Correlated Volatility Factor (CVF) is	The Envelope Factor (EF) is
	Pts.
1	2.20
2	2.30
3	2.40
4	2.50
5	2.65
6	2.80
7	2.95
8	3.10
9	3.25
10	3.40
11	3.60
12	3.80
13	4.00
14	4.20
15	4.40
16	4.65
17	4.90
18	5.15
19	5.40
20	5.70
21	6.00

PLATINUM ENVELOPE FACTORS

If Correlated Volatility Factor (CVF) is	The Envelope Factor (EF) is
	US$
1	14.30
2	15.10
3	15.90
4	16.70
5	17.60
6	18.50
7	19.50
8	20.50
9	21.60
10	22.80
11	24.00
12	25.20
13	26.50
14	27.90
15	29.40
16	31.00
17	32.60
18	34.30
19	36.10
20	38.00
21	40.00

PORK BELLY ENVELOPE FACTORS

If Correlated Volatility Factor (CVF) is	The Envelope Factor (EF) is
	Pts.
1	1.42
2	1.50
3	1.57
4	1.65
5	1.75
6	1.85
7	1.95
8	2.05
9	2.15
10	2.27
11	2.40
12	2.52
13	2.65
14	2.80
15	2.95
16	3.10
17	3.25
18	3.42
19	3.60
20	3.80
21	4.00

SILVER ENVELOPE FACTORS

If Correlated Volatility Factor (CVF) is	The Envelope Factor (EF) is
	US¢
1	35.80
2	37.70
3	39.70
4	41.80
5	44.00
6	46.30
7	48.70
8	51.30
9	54.00
10	56.90
11	59.90
12	63.00
13	66.30
14	69.80
15	73.50
16	77.40
17	81.50
18	85.70
19	90.30
20	95.00
21	100.00

SOYBEANS* ENVELOPE FACTORS

If Correlated Volatility Factor (CVF) is	The Envelope Factor (EF) is
	US¢
1	21.50
2	22.75
3	23.75
4	25.00
5	26.25
6	27.75
7	29.25
8	30.75
9	32.50
10	34.25
11	36.00
12	37.75
13	39.75
14	41.75
15	44.00
16	46.50
17	49.00
18	51.50
19	54.25
20	57.00
21	60.00

* Soybean prices are quoted in fractions of cents, rather than in decimals, but for purposes of computation, these fractions are converted into decimals.

SOYBEAN MEAL ENVELOPE FACTORS

If Correlated Volatility Factor (CVF) is	The Envelope Factor (EF) is
	US$
1	7.20
2	7.60
3	8.00
4	8.40
5	8.80
6	9.30
7	9.80
8	10.30
9	10.80
10	11.40
11	12.00
12	12.60
13	13.30
14	14.00
15	14.70
16	15.50
17	16.30
18	17.20
19	18.10
20	19.00
21	20.00

SUGAR (WORLD) ENVELOPE FACTORS

If Correlated Volatility Factor (CVF) is	The Envelope Factor (EF) is
	Pts.
1	0.36
2	0.38
3	0.40
4	0.42
5	0.44
6	0.46
7	0.48
8	0.51
9	0.54
10	0.57
11	0.60
12	0.63
13	0.66
14	0.69
15	0.73
16	0.77
17	0.81
18	0.86
19	0.90
20	0.95
21	1.00

TREASURY BILLS ENVELOPE FACTORS

If Correlated Volatility Factor (CVF) is	The Envelope Factor (EF) is
	Pts.
1	0.43
2	0.45
3	0.47
4	0.50
5	0.53
6	0.56
7	0.59
8	0.62
9	0.65
10	0.68
11	0.72
12	0.76
13	0.80
14	0.84
15	0.88
16	0.93
17	0.98
18	1.03
19	1.08
20	1.14
21	1.20

To use the Envelope Factor (EF), if you have a *long* position in the market, just *subtract* the appropriate EF from the TI to obtain the MTN for both offsetting your long position and simultaneously going short.

If you have a *short* position in the market, just *add* the EF to the TI to obtain the MTN for both covering your short position and simultaneously going long.

As an actual application of the EF, let us once again refer to our July 1980 Copper and to the three TI's that we have previously calculated; that is, for August 22, 23, and 24 of 1979.

Referring to the Copper Envelope Factors table, we find that the CVF of 6 for August 22 calls for an EF of 4.65. At this point, August 22, we have no position in the market and, therefore, must look at the closing price of August 22 to determine where the market is, in relationship to our TI. The closing price of August 22 was 88.60, .59 below our 89.19 TI of August 22 (to be used for trading on August 23). Adding the EF of 4.65 to our 89.19 TI gives us our MTN to go *long* at 93.84 (always round off to the nearest minimum trading increment of the futures contract being traded). After rounding, our signal for actual market use would then be 93.85. Also, we would subtract the 4.65 from the 89.19 to see if August 22nd's closing price might fall within the trading envelope, and we discover that it does, since our MTN to go *short* is 84.54 (84.55). Therefore, on August 23 (the first attempt at market entry), we must enter orders to go long *or* short since August 22nd's closing price of 88.60 is *within* the envelope. Please refer to Figure 5 for a graphic illustration of this actual example.

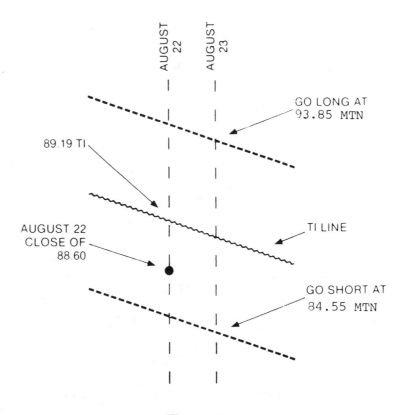

Figure 5
Initial Market Entry
(Market Close Within Both MTN's)

49

The System

The other situation that can occur on the first attempt at market entry is if the previous day's closing price is *outside* of the trading envelope; that is, if the close of August 22 had been above our MTN of 93.85, or below our MTN of 84.55:

1. If the closing price, let us say, had been 94.20 (instead of the actual 88.60) on August 22, above the 93.85 MTN, you would assume that you were already in a long position and could only go short. Therefore, the only order you would enter would be to go short at the lower MTN of 84.55 (See Figure 6).

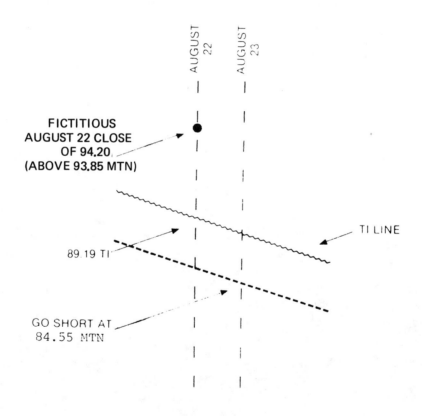

Figure 6
Initial Market Entry
(Market Close Above Upper MTN)

2. Conversely, if the closing price had been 83.00 on August 22, below the 84.55 MTN, you would assume that you were already in a short position and could only go long. Therefore, the only order you would enter would be to go long at the upper MTN of 93.85 (See Figure 7).

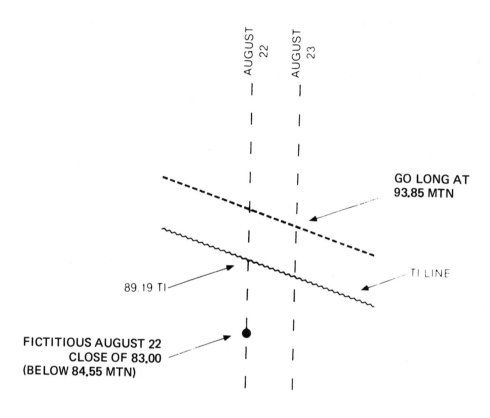

Figure 7
Initial Market Entry
(Market Close Below Lower MTN)

There is no guarantee that your MTN will be reached by the market on the first attempt at market entry, or for any number of days thereafter. Therefore, each day you must enter your orders at the newly calculated MTN's until market entry is achieved. From that point, you will be either long or short continuously in the market.

Once you have established the routine of making your calculations each day, it becomes a simple and automatic process to arrive at your MTN for the next day's trading.

Chapter Two

Application of The Maxtrend System To The Actual Market

Now that you know how to arrive at the Master Trading Number (MTN), you must learn when and how to trade with it in the futures market.

CHOOSING THE FUTURES CONTRACT MONTH TO TRADE

Normally, you will trade in the nearest futures contract month. The reasons—truer market action and a higher volume of trading; hence, more market liquidity and better trade execution. As an example, trading in copper, if it is late April or May, you would commence trading in July Copper. If it were in June or July, you would commence trading in September Copper, etc.

WHEN TO STOP TRADING IN THE FUTURES CONTRACT MONTH YOU ARE TRADING

You should usually stop trading in the futures contract month you are trading one day to four weeks before its *first notice day* (when you can actually receive notice to become involved in physical delivery of the future). Your broker, or the futures exchange itself, can tell you when the first notice day is for the futures contract you are trading. First notice days can vary from future to future.

Application of The Maxtrend System to the Actual Market

As an example, we close out our last trade in July 1980 Copper toward the end of May 1980, approximately five weeks before its first notice day. Because it is so close to the first notice day, rather than institute a new trade in the July 1980 Copper, we begin to trade in September 1980 Copper.

If you are still in an incompleted (open) position and the first notice day is imminent, close out your existing position on the close of the market on the day before the first notice day. At exactly the same time (at the close of the market on the day before the first notice day) reinstate the same position in the next furthest out contract month.

As an example, if you were in a long position in May Copper and the first notice day arrived (last trading day of April), you would close out your long May position at the close of the market on that day, and at the same time buy (go long) a July contract to keep the trade continuous.

Note: Begin computing the MTN for a further out contract month approximately four weeks before the first notice day of the contract month you are trading. You do this to be ready to commence trading in the further out contract month exactly at the same time that you close out your last trade of the contract month in which you are currently trading. This means, for a few days or weeks, you will have to compute two MTN's each day for each future, one for the contract month you are trading, the other for the contract month you plan to trade.

HOW AND WHEN TO PLACE YOUR TRADING ORDERS AND WHAT TRADING ORDERS TO USE

There are only two orders used when trading under The Maxtrend System, the "stop" order and the "stop-close only" order. Both are similar, the only difference being that the "stop" order is executed immediately upon the "stop" price being touched or penetrated by market action; the "stop-close only" order is only executed upon the "stop" price being touched (or penetrated) by market action when the market closes. The straight "stop" order is used only with three commodities in the portfolio: copper, pork bellies, and sugar. The remaining 10 commodities use only the "stop-close only" order. These orders are used to get into, and to get out of, the market.

Note: Remember, our MTN is always above the current market price when we wish to buy, and always below it when we wish to sell, necessitating the use of the "stop" order. If we do not use the word "stop" in our order, our order will be executed immediately, instead of at the designated buy or sell price (the MTN's).

As an example, let us once again use our July 1980 Copper, which uses a straight "stop" order. On May 23, 1980, our 94.95 (MTN) Stop Order was touched to establish a "long" position. Now, assuming we are trading only one contract at a time, we already were in a "short" position from the previous signal of February 20, 1980; therefore, our order at 94.95 Stop would have to be for buying two July 1980 Copper, instead of one. The reason is that we must offset our one existing "short" position and also establish one new "long" position. Whenever we offset a position, we change direction (this is called "reversing"), which leads to the fact that once we begin to trade a future, we are always in the market with it, either "long" or "short."

Please understand that you can increase or decrease the number of contracts you wish to trade at any time, but always make sure that you trade enough contracts to cover your present position, and to reverse your position for at least one contract, or more. The only exceptions to "reversing" are, 1) when we first enter the market for a future we must only put in an order for one contract (assuming we are trading only one contract) as it is our initial position and, 2) when exiting a particular contract month for a future we must enter an order to just offset the trade from that month and put another order in for the new position in the next contract month.

With straight "stop" orders, make sure your orders are placed *before the market opens* each day. For "stop-close only" orders, make sure your orders are placed *before the market closes* each day.

Remember, for your initial entry into the market, you may spend days or weeks of putting in orders each day without getting your MTN touched. Be patient, once your first trade has been executed in a future, you will be in it for as long as you desire.

MONEY MANAGEMENT

Money management can run the gamut from very complex and sophisticated risk distribution and portfolio balancing criteria, to a very simplistic, "Let's buy a few and see what happens."

There is nothing esoteric about money management when using The Maxtrend

System—there are just three rules; two of them are just about standard in the industry, the third is new and tailored specifically for Maxtrend.

Rule 1. Don't put more than 10 to 15% of your total trading capital into any one future.

Rule 2. Don't put more than 50 to 55% of your total futures trading capital into actual trades at any one time.

Rule 3. If you have had four losing trades in a row in the same future, double the number of contracts you are trading for the fifth trade and beyond until you have had a winning trade, then go back to the original number of contracts. *This rule is optional, and although not perfect, has proven to be extremely effective when using Maxtrend.*

Assume we are trading just one contract. As an actual example, silver futures suffered four straight losing trades from September 9, 1982 to December 12, 1982, but on the next trade, it garnered a profit of 301.4 cents ($15,070) on February 2, 1983. Being the fifth trade, and using Rule 3, the profit on the trade would have been 602.8 cents ($30,140).

Using Rule 3 during the 7-year historical performance study with all 13 commodities increased the Total Net Profit of the system significantly.

The rationale behind Rule 3 is that a well performing, trend-following system such as The Maxtrend System will very rarely have more than five or six losing trades in a row before having a winning trade. In actuality, all testing done on Maxtrend has shown no more than eight losers in a row. Remember, though, you will be increasing your capital requirements by a factor of two if you decide to utilize Rule 3, so make sure that you have adequate trading funds to perform under Rule 3 before using it.

FOUR IMPORTANT THINGS TO REMEMBER

1. Devote the necessary time, effort and study to learning and applying The Maxtrend System as you would to any other serious business venture—it's *your money.*

2. Adhere to every instruction stated in Maxtrend; do not deviate from those instructions or the value of this highly researched trading method will be lost.

3. Be willing to accept a possible series of losses with the knowledge that one good profitable trade can usually offset all the losing trades.

4. Be totally automatic in your trading. Put your orders in and forget about them. If a trade is made, a trade is made. In this way, your trading will be unclouded and concise. Depend fully on Maxtrend and its principles.

Glossary of Abbreviations

So as to make it easy for you to learn the few important abbreviations used in this book and to give you one place at which to refer to them, the following is an alphabetical list of those abbreviations and their meanings.

ADAR	=	Average Daily Actual Range
ARO	=	Actual Range One
ARVF	=	Actual Range Volatility Factor
CF	=	Constant Factor
CVF	=	Correlated Volatility Factor
DPA	=	Daily Price Average
EF	=	Envelope Factor
MTN	=	Master Trading Number
PADAR	=	Previous Average Daily Actual Range
PDR	=	Price Differential Range
PDVF	=	Price Differential Volatility Factor
TI	=	Trend Indicator

The Maxtrend System
7-Year Performance Record

Performance By Each
Individual Futures Contract—
Trade-By-Trade

COFFEE

DELIV	RULE	POSITION	DATE-IN	PRICE-IN	DATE-OUT	PRICE-OUT	MAX-LOSS	DAYS	MAX-GAIN	DAYS	NET-PROFIT	DAYS	
7-78	M	SHORT	1-24-78	163.1000	3-28-78	147.8600	806-	12	12037	29	5650	42	S
7-78	M	LONG	3-28-78	147.8600	6-12-78	165.5000	2205-	6	14490	49	6550	54	L
7-78	M END	SHORT	6-12-78	165.5000	6-30-78	158.3800	1687-	4	2718	6	2605	16	S
12-78	ENDM	SHORT	7-3-78	132.5000	7-31-78	121.1700	187-	1	12225	16	4183	19	S
12-78	M	LONG	7-31-78	121.1700	11-15-78	144.0000	4376-	3	13811	49	8496	75	L
12-78	M END	SHORT	11-15-78	144.0000	11-30-78	141.7500	1462-	7	2126	3	778	12	S
12-78	ENDM	SHORT	11-30-78	128.2500	12-26-78	129.2500	375-	17	5156	10	440-	17	S
7-79	M	LONG	12-26-78	129.2500	1-11-79	124.1600	1908-	12	1500	7	1973-	12	L
7-79	M	SHORT	1-11-79	124.1600	3-5-79	132.2000	3015-	37	1698	26	3080-	37	S
7-79	M END	LONG	3-5-79	132.2000	6-29-79	215.2300	1106-	37	31425	83	31071	84	L
12-79	ENDM	LONG	6-29-79	220.0000	7-13-79	203.3200	6292-	9	0	1	6357-	9	L
12-79	M	SHORT	7-13-79	203.3200	8-15-79	195.3400	2943-	6	7488	18	2890	24	S
12-79	M	LONG	8-15-79	195.3400	10-12-79	208.1800	1608-	1	10372	34	4750	42	L
12-79	M	SHORT	10-12-79	208.1800	10-19-79	216.9800	3300-	6	2317	5	3365-	6	S
12-79	M END	LONG	10-19-79	216.9800	11-30-79	220.0900	5805-	1	1882	30	1101	31	L
7-80	ENDM	LONG	11-30-79	189.6000	2-19-80	185.6000	1500-	1	0	1	1565-	1	L
7-80	M	SHORT	2-19-80	185.6000	3-28-80	179.6400	1500-	2	5850	21	2170	52	S
7-80	M	LONG	3-28-80	179.6400	5-5-80	189.1600	990-	1	7353	15	3505	29	L
7-80	M	SHORT	5-5-80	189.1600	6-16-80	194.9400	2167-	26	2497	24	2232	26	S
7-80	M END	LONG	6-16-80	194.9400	6-30-80	182.6100	4623-	30	3585	10	4688	30	L
12-80	ENDM	SHORT	6-30-80	181.8100	8-25-80	168.0500	2396-	1	6885	6	5395	12	S
12-80	M	LONG	8-25-80	156.0200	9-9-80	156.0200	446-	14	16815	24	9606	26	L
12-80	M	SHORT	9-9-80	143.3400	9-15-80	143.3400	7413-	11	930	2	2723	14	S
12-80	M	LONG	9-15-80	130.2600	11-28-80	130.2600	2658-	5	1998	6	4970-	11	L
12-80	M END	SHORT	11-28-80	124.4500	12-29-80	114.7500	4905-	2	1147	2	5751	5	S
7-81	ENDM	LONG	12-29-80	130.4600	1-26-81	130.4600	2062-	19	10560	46	2318-	54	L
7-81	M	SHORT	1-26-81	125.3500	6-30-81	125.3500	2253-	19	2606	10	1981-	59	S
7-81	M	SHORT	6-30-81	89.0500	7-13-81	93.6200	1916-	6	2808	11	11833	19	S
7-81	M END	LONG	7-13-81	95.6000	8-5-81	95.6000	2306-	8	14943	107	2521-	110	L
12-81	ENDM	SHORT	8-5-81	95.6000	9-11-81	108.0900	2456-	3	1987	5	4618	8	S
12-81	M	LONG	9-11-81	108.0900	11-24-81	115.7500	1687-	10	12033	13	2937-	18	L
12-81	M	SHORT	11-24-81	115.7500	11-30-81	139.6600	4203-	4	4815	20	8901	27	S
12-81	M	LONG	11-30-81	139.6600	1-5-82	136.6100	1293-	1	14812	39	1078	53	L
12-81	M END	SHORT	1-5-82	125.0000	3-16-82	134.2500	1252-	23	1503	4	3533-	5	S
7-82	ENDM	SHORT	3-16-82	134.2500	5-26-82	127.2700	3468-	14	1500	1	2682-	23	S
7-82	M	LONG	5-26-82	127.2700	6-30-82	132.8900	2812-	51	2156	27	2172-	50	L
7-82	M	LONG	6-30-82	132.8900	7-6-82	140.6000	2107-	1	3926	25	2826	51	L
7-82	M END	LONG	7-6-82	127.4600	8-5-82	118.0200	1552-	3	3510	8	3605-	26	L
12-82	ENDM	LONG	8-5-82	118.0200	11-1-82	135.0200	3540-	23	0	1	1677-	3	L
12-82	M	LONG	11-1-82	122.3200	11-30-82	136.6500	1612-	4	2445	16	4697	23	L
12-82	M	SHORT	11-30-82	135.0200	5-16-83	129.4800	1395-	16	8823	41	676-	62	S
12-82	M	SHORT	5-16-83	128.0600	6-30-83	124.6300	2805-	115	570	4	597	21	S
12-82	M END	SHORT	6-30-83	129.4800	11-30-83	150.7800	532-	33	3922	55	1883-	115	S
7-83	ENDM	LONG	11-30-83	125.1900	2-7-84	130.7900	2336-	47	2257	9	9531	34	L
7-83	M END	LONG	2-7-84	136.0000	5-11-84	151.7400	52-	67	9735	106	2018-	107	L
12-83	ENDM	SHORT	5-11-84	130.7900	5-25-84	145.0600	1953-	11	1725	10	7921-	47	S
7-84	ENDM	LONG	5-25-84	151.7400	6-27-84	152.7500	7856-	23	352	2	2570-	67	L
7-84	M	LONG	6-27-84	145.0600	6-29-84	149.5000	2505-	3	2505	7	2948-	11	L
7-84	M	LONG	6-29-84	152.7500	7-11-84	137.0600	2883-	7	1410	7	1283-	23	L
7-84	M END	LONG	7-11-84	140.3500	8-10-84	142.2900	1950-	23	86	1	1298-	4	L
7-84	ENDM	SHORT	8-10-84	137.0600	9-12-84	139.6100	1233-	23	1173	3	2026-	7	S
12-84	M	SHORT	9-12-84	142.2900	11-12-84	143.8600	1961-	23	566	14	1070-	23	S
12-84	M	SHORT	11-12-84	139.6100	11-30-84	143.5400	1005-	44	2816	13	1538-	44	S
12-84	M END	LONG	11-12-84	143.5400	11-30-84	138.8600	1473-	14	2403	14	1820-	15	L
12-84	END	LONG	—	—	—	—	2021-	10	397	2	—	2	L

COFFEE

DELIV	RULE	POSITION	DATE-IN	PRICE-IN	DATE-OUT	PRICE-OUT	MAX-LOSS	DAYS	MAX-GAIN	DAYS	NET-PROFIT	DAYS	
7-85	ENDM	LONG	12-3-84	134.7600	4-12-85	139.2900	172-	5	4740	43	1633	89	L
7-85	M M	SHORT	4-12-85	139.2900	4-24-85	146.6900	2775-	9	315	5	2840-	9	S
7-85	M END	LONG	4-24-85	146.6900	4-26-85	146.4800	1087-	1	210	2	143-	4	L

TOTALS FOR ALL CONTRACTS OF: COFFEE

NET PROFIT = 46690	NUM TRADES = 58	LARGEST PROFIT = 31071	AV PROFIT TRADE= 6070	REL PROFIT FACTOR= .88
TOTAL PROFITS = 139618	NUM WINS = 23	LARGEST LOSS = 7921-	AV LOSS TRADE= 2655-	AV PROFIT/AV LOSS= 2.28
TOTAL LOSSES = 92928-	NUM LOSSES = 35	BEST POSITION = 31425	AV DAYS IN WIN = 45	MAX WINS IN ROW= 6
PROFIT FACTOR = 1.50	PERCENT WINS = 40	WORST POSITION = 7856-	AV DAYS IN LOSS= 24	MAX LOSSES IN ROW= 10
MAX DRAWDOWN = 25842-	MARGIN = 1500	AV BEST POSITION= 5145	NUM MONTHS = 87	DAY COMMISSION = 65
AV NET PROFIT = 805	RETURN ON CAP= 18	AV WORST POSITION= 2201-	PROFIT/DRAWDOWN= 1.80	NIGHT COMMISSION = 65

64

COPPER

DELIV	RULE	POSITION	DATE-IN	PRICE-IN	DATE-OUT	PRICE-OUT	MAX-LOSS	DAYS	MAX-GAIN	DAYS	NET-PROFIT	DAYS	
9-78	M END	LONG	5-25-78	66.0332	8-31-78	63.4000	1708-	25	441	4	723-	70	L
3-79	ENDEND	LONG	8-31-78	66.7500	2-28-79	91.3500	262-	4	6312	123	6085	124	L
9-79	ENDM	LONG	2-28-79	93.1500	5- 8-79	85.6492	1962-	8	1537	28	1940-	48	L
9-79	M	SHORT	5- 8-79	85.6492	8-15-79	90.4552	1201-	70	1837	39	1266-	70	S
9-79	M END	LONG	8-15-79	90.4552	8-31-79	90.0000	1238-	7	311	12	178-	14	L
3-80	ENDM	LONG	8-31-79	92.9500	10-16-79	89.0389	1687-	11	6262	21	1042-	31	L
3-80	M	SHORT	10-16-79	89.0389	11-19-79	101.1063	3016-	25	434	2	3081-	25	S
3-80	M MO	LONG	11-19-79	101.1063	11-19-79	123.7000	2101-	6	11348	58	5583	63	L
3-80	MO END	SHORT	2-20-80	123.7000	2-29-80	119.5000	1325-	2	1675	5	985	9	S
9-80	ENDM	SHORT	2-29-80	128.0000	5-23-80	96.5593	100-	1	9875	35	7795	59	S
9-80	M	LONG	5-23-80	96.5593	6-10-80	87.0528	2376-	12	322	2	2441-	12	L
9-80	M	SHORT	6-10-80	87.0528	6-30-80	93.9482	1723-	15	638	2	1788-	15	S
9-80	M	LONG	6-30-80	93.9482	7-30-80	94.8086	537-	2	2950	17	150	22	L
9-80	M END	SHORT	7-30-80	94.8086	8-29-80	87.2000	1397-	12	2727	22	1837	24	S
3-81	ENDM	SHORT	8-29-80	92.6500	9-11-80	100.5421	1973-	8	112	2	2038-	8	S
3-81	M	LONG	9-11-80	100.5421	9-29-80	93.7490	1698-	13	1189	9	1763-	13	L
3-81	M END	SHORT	9-29-80	93.7490	2-27-81	80.1500	1787-	20	3687	96	3334	105	S
9-81	ENDM	SHORT	2-27-81	87.3500	7-31-81	83.5294	1262-	19	2787	88	890	107	S
9-81	M	LONG	7-31-81	83.5294	8-25-81	76.8093	1680-	18	492	9	1745-	18	L
9-81	M END	SHORT	8-25-81	76.8093	8-31-81	77.4000	510-	4	377	1	212-	6	S
3-82	ENDEND	SHORT	8-31-81	85.1000	2-26-82	69.1500	475-	10	3987	125	3922	125	S
9-82	ENDM	SHORT	2-26-82	75.1000	7-20-82	67.9982	325-	47	5100	79	1685	99	S
9-82	M MO	LONG	7-20-82	67.9982	8- 9-82	59.6000	2099-	15	425	2	2164-	15	L
9-82	MO END	SHORT	8- 9-82	59.6000	8-31-82	62.5000	1650-	11	475	3	790-	18	S
3-83	ENDM	SHORT	8-31-82	66.1000	10-14-82	69.8563	1162-	4	1337	23	1004-	31	S
3-83	M	LONG	10-14-82	69.8563	2-28-83	73.6500	1651-	29	2485	92	883	94	L
9-83	M END	LONG	2-28-83	78.0000	3- 4-83	75.6101	597-	4	812	3	662-	4	L
9-83	M END	SHORT	3- 4-83	75.6101	8-31-83	71.6500	1872-	43	1065	122	925	123	S
3-84	ENDEND	SHORT	8-31-83	76.1000	2-29-84	64.9500	375-	7	3712	95	2722	126	S
9-84	ENDEND	SHORT	2-29-84	68.7500	8-31-84	61.1500	1412-	22	3012	106	1835	130	S
3-85	ENDEND	SHORT	8-31-84	64.9500	2-28-85	58.6500	0	1	2362	78	1510	124	S

TOTALS FOR ALL CONTRACTS OF: COPPER

NET PROFIT = 17304	NUM TRADES = 31	LARGEST PROFIT = 7795	AV PROFIT TRADE= 2676	REL PROFIT FACTOR= .89
TOTAL PROFITS = 40141	NUM WINS = 15	LARGEST LOSS = 3081-	AV LOSS TRADE= 1427-	AV PROFIT/AV LOSS= 1.87
TOTAL LOSSES = 22837-	NUM LOSSES = 16	BEST POSITION = 11348	AV DAYS IN WIN = 89	MAX WINS IN ROW= 4
PROFIT FACTOR = 1.75	PERCENT WINS = 48	WORST POSITION = 3016-	AV DAYS IN LOSS= 25	MAX LOSSES IN ROW= 5
MAX DRAWDOWN = 7507-	MARGIN = 800	AV BEST POSITION= 2666	NUM MONTHS = 65	DAY COMMISSION = 65
AV NET PROFIT = 558	RETURN ON CAP= 24	AV WORST POSITION= 1242-	PROFIT/DRAWDOWN= 2.30	NIGHT COMMISSION = 65

65

COMEX GOLD

DELIV	RULE	POSITION	DATE-IN	PRICE-IN	DATE-OUT	PRICE-OUT	MAX-LOSS	DAYS	MAX-GAIN	DAYS	NET-PROFIT	DAYS	
2-80	M M	LONG	9-10-79	355.3000	1-24-80	684.0000	930-	4	51770	92	32805	95	L
2-80	M END	SHORT	1-24-80	684.0000	1-31-80	681.5000	3900-	1	7700	3	185	7	S
8-80	ENDM	SHORT	1-31-80	748.0000	5-30-80	555.0000	4390-	7	25600	32	19235	83	L
8-80	M	LONG	5-30-80	555.0000	7-15-80	620.5000	1400-	1	14100	27	6485	32	S
8-80	M END	SHORT	7-15-80	620.5000	7-31-80	619.7000	3450-	9	1650	4	15	14	S
2-81	ENDM	SHORT	7-31-80	654.7000	9- 8-80	711.2000	5650-	26	2370	8	5715-	26	S
2-81	M	LONG	9- 8-80	711.2000	10-23-80	650.7000	6050-	34	5780	12	6115-	34	L
2-81	M END	SHORT	10-23-80	650.7000	1-30-81	501.7000	3330-	9	16570	66	14835	68	S
8-81	ENDM	SHORT	1-30-81	538.4000	3-20-81	558.4000	2040-	34	6400	22	2105-	34	S
8-81	M	LONG	3-20-81	558.4000	4-13-81	499.4000	5900-	17	2280	5	5965-	17	L
8-81	M END	SHORT	4-13-81	499.4000	7-31-81	403.5000	2310-	7	10240	60	9525	78	S
2-82	ENDM	SHORT	7-31-81	433.7000	8-18-81	466.9000	3320-	12	1870	2	3385-	12	S
2-82	M	LONG	8-18-81	466.9000	11-10-81	422.7000	4420-	60	2830	24	4485-	60	L
2-82	M END	SHORT	11-10-81	422.7000	1-29-82	384.6000	1430-	18	5370	49	3745	57	S
8-82	ENDM	SHORT	1-29-82	409.5000	4- 6-82	375.7000	350-	4	8250	30	3315	46	S
8-82	M	LONG	4- 6-82	375.7000	7-30-82	342.7000	7820-	53	1030	6	3365-	82	L
8-82	M END	SHORT	7-30-82	362.9000	9-29-82	407.0000	1440-	7	15510	27	4345	42	L
2-83	ENDM	SHORT	9-29-82	407.0000	10-13-82	466.7000	5970-	11	1100	4	6035-	11	S
2-83	M	LONG	10-13-82	466.7000	1-31-83	510.1000	6270-	22	4430	75	4275	76	L
8-83	M END	LONG	1-31-83	534.6000	2-23-83	485.8000	4880-	16	140	11	4945-	16	L
8-83	M END	SHORT	2-23-83	485.8000	7-29-83	412.8000	870-	2	8480	72	7235	111	S
2-84	ENDEND	SHORT	7-29-83	435.3000	1-31-84	373.8000	1340-	17	7280	125	6085	129	S
8-84	ENDEND	SHORT	1-31-84	391.6000	7-31-84	337.7000	3290-	23	5960	124	5325	127	S
2-85	ENDEND	SHORT	7-31-84	357.3000	1-31-85	304.1000	2020-	16	6060	109	5255	128	S

TOTALS FOR ALL CONTRACTS OF: COMEX GOLD

NET PROFIT = 80550	NUM TRADES = 24	LARGEST PROFIT = 32805	AV PROFIT TRADE= 8177	REL PROFIT FACTOR= 1.07
TOTAL PROFITS = 122665	NUM WINS = 15	LARGEST LOSS = 6115-	AV LOSS TRADE= 4679-	AV PROFIT/AV LOSS= 1.74
TOTAL LOSSES = 42115-	NUM LOSSES = 9	BEST POSITION = 51770	AV DAYS IN WIN = 73	MAX WINS IN ROW= 5
PROFIT FACTOR = 2.91	PERCENT WINS = 63	WORST POSITION = 7820-	AV DAYS IN LOSS= 32	MAX LOSSES IN ROW= 2
MAX DRAWDOWN = 11830-	MARGIN = 1200	AV BEST POSITION= 9363	NUM MONTHS= 58	DAY COMMISSION = 65
AV NET PROFIT = 3356	RETURN ON CAP= 80	AV WORST POSITION= 2941-	PROFIT/DRAWDOWN= 6.80	NIGHT COMMISSION = 65

HEATING OIL #2

DELIV	RULE	POSITION	DATE-IN	PRICE-IN	PRICE-OUT	DATE-OUT	MAX-LOSS	DAYS	MAX-GAIN	DAYS	NET-PROFIT	DAYS	
8-80	M	LONG	1-30-80	90.5000	82.6000	2-13-80	3318-	11	210	2	3383-	11	L
8-80	M	SHORT	2-13-80	82.6000	82.0000	4-3-80	504-	11	2142	20	187	36	S
8-80	M	LONG	4-3-80	82.0000	78.1000	6-16-80	1638-	51	525	17	1703-	51	L
8-80	M END	SHORT	6-16-80	78.1000	76.8400	6-30-80	42-	1	546	11	464	12	S
2-81	ENDM	SHORT	6-30-80	88.5000	86.4400	9-23-80	0	1	3738	28	800	58	S
2-81	M	LONG	9-23-80	86.4400	94.5700	12-8-80	1087-	4	6535	40	3349	53	L
2-81	M END	SHORT	12-8-80	94.5700	99.1500	12-31-80	1986-	16	1121	4	1988-	17	S
8-81	ENDM	LONG	12-31-80	99.1500	106.3000	2-5-81	0	1	210	1	145	1	L
8-81	M	SHORT	2-5-81	106.3000	106.3000	2-9-81	840-	2	126	1	905-	2	S
8-81	M	LONG	2-9-81	104.3000	100.2500	4-6-81	849-	1	3066	25	1636	40	L
8-81	M	SHORT	4-6-81	100.2500	95.2000	4-23-81	2121-	13	231	3	2186-	13	S
8-81	M END	SHORT	4-23-81	95.2000	92.0500	6-30-81	231-	32	2121	32	1258	49	S
2-82	ENDM	LONG	7-10-81	101.2000	103.0000	8-24-81	756-	7	147	7	821-	32	L
2-82	M	SHORT	8-24-81	103.0000	101.4700	10-15-81	642-	32	840	7	707	38	S
2-82	M	LONG	10-15-81	101.4700	102.6000	12-9-81	474-	38	1457	12	539-	39	L
2-82	M	SHORT	12-9-81	102.6000	100.2100	12-31-81	1003-	39	336	16	1068-	16	S
2-82	M END	SHORT	12-31-81	100.2100	96.7000	3-25-82	121-	1	1516	15	1409	58	S
8-82	ENDM	LONG	3-25-82	93.0000	75.0000	6-1-82	462-	1	10080	46	7495	47	L
8-82	M	SHORT	6-1-82	75.0300	90.0700	6-8-82	2289-	6	8400	41	6264	6	L
8-82	M	LONG	6-8-82	90.0700	95.5200	6-17-82	2494-	8	659	2	2354-	8	S
8-82	M	SHORT	6-17-82	95.5200	89.5800	6-30-82	806-	8	495	6	2559-	11	L
8-82	M END	SHORT	6-30-82	89.5800	94.5000	8-9-82	1260-	27	978	8	98	27	S
2-83	ENDM	LONG	8-9-82	91.5000	94.5000	10-27-82	1596-	7	777	8	1325	57	L
2-83	M	SHORT	10-27-82	94.5000	97.2700	12-9-82	978-	50	3738	50	1098	30	S
2-83	M	LONG	12-9-82	97.2700	88.3600	12-21-82	2385-	26	7400	26	3677	9	L
2-83	M	SHORT	12-21-82	88.3600	82.6800	1-6-83	907-	9	646	9	2450-	8	S
2-83	M END	SHORT	1-6-83	82.6800	78.3000	3-15-83	1155-	6	705	4	749-	47	L
8-83	ENDM	LONG	3-15-83	78.3000	73.6800	4-14-83	999-	11	4494	33	1875	23	L
8-83	M END	LONG	8-4-83	88.4600	85.3500	8-31-83	1306-	5	2864	20	2366	19	L
2-84	ENDM	SHORT	8-31-83	85.3500	81.7300	12-23-83	483-	19	310	7	1371-	80	L
2-84	M	LONG	12-23-83	81.7300	82.6500	12-30-83	621-	15	4410	75	1455	6	L
2-84	M	LONG	4-23-84	79.3000	79.6700	6-8-84	735-	1	1163	2	321	33	L
2-84	M END	LONG	6-8-84	79.6700	77.9500	6-29-84	348-	5	1974	24	90	17	L
8-84	ENDM	SHORT	6-29-84	81.8500	79.3000	7-11-84	63-	11	1751	11	657	29	L
8-84	M	SHORT	7-11-84	79.9500	77.9500	8-21-84	735-	13	2604	13	128-	38	S
2-85	M	LONG	8-21-84	82.0000	80.5800	10-12-84	609-	26	1617	26	661-	38	L
2-85	M END	SHORT	10-12-84	80.5800	73.3200	12-28-84	239-	1	3204	48	2984	53	S

TOTALS FOR ALL CONTRACTS OF: HEATING OIL #2

NET PROFIT = 12731	NUM TRADES = 37	LARGEST PROFIT = 7495	AV PROFIT TRADE= 1881	REL PROFIT FACTOR= .69	
TOTAL PROFITS = 37628	NUM WINS = 20	LARGEST LOSS = 3383-	AV LOSS TRADE= 1464-	AV PROFIT/AV LOSS= 1.28	
TOTAL LOSSES = 24897-	NUM LOSSES = 17	BEST POSITION = 10080	AV DAYS IN WIN= 36	MAX WINS IN ROW= 4	
PROFIT FACTOR = 1.51	PERCENT WINS = 54	WORST POSITION = 3318-	AV DAYS IN LOSS= 21	MAX LOSSES IN ROW= 4	
MAX DRAWDOWN = 6140-	MARGIN = 2000	AV BEST POSITION= 2335	NUM MONTHS = 57	DAY COMMISSION = 65	
AV NET PROFIT = 344	RETURN ON CAP= 23	AV WORST POSITION= 864-	PROFIT/DRAWDOWN= 2.07	NIGHT COMMISSION= 65	

67

JAPANESE YEN

DELIV	RULE	POSITION	DATE-IN	PRICE-IN	DATE-OUT	PRICE-OUT	MAX-LOSS	DAYS	MAX-GAIN	DAYS	NET-PROFIT	DAYS	L/S
6-78	M M	LONG	3-16-78	.4388	4-21-78	.4448	162-	1	3300	12	685	26	L
6-78	M M	SHORT	4-21-78	.4448	5-31-78	.4560	1400-	28	975	22	1465-	28	S
6-78	M END	LONG	5-31-78	.4560	5-31-78	.4560	587-	1	25	1	65-	2	L
9-78	ENDEND	LONG	5-31-78	.4624	8-31-78	.5225	675-	3	11037	54	7447	66	L
12-78	ENDM	LONG	8-31-78	.5311	11-2-78	.5379	750-	5	5300	41	785	44	L
12-78	M END	SHORT	11-2-78	.5379	11-30-78	.5048	450-	5	4387	18	4072	19	S
3-79	ENDEND	SHORT	11-30-78	.5167	2-28-79	.4969	1975-	19	2700	61	2410	62	S
6-79	ENDM	SHORT	2-28-79	.5046	5-9-79	.4728	0	1	7262	44	3910	49	S
6-79	M M	LONG	5-9-79	.4728	5-29-79	.4513	2687-	14	400	3	2752-	14	L
6-79	M END	SHORT	5-29-79	.4513	5-31-79	.4539	1000-	2	37	1	390-	4	S
9-79	ENDM	SHORT	5-29-79	.4590	6-25-79	.4752	2025-	17	187	1	2090-	17	S
9-79	M M	LONG	6-25-79	.4752	8-29-79	.4506	3075-	47	275	1	3140-	47	L
9-79	M END	SHORT	8-29-79	.4506	8-31-79	.4570	862-	3	12	1	865-	4	S
12-79	ENDEND	SHORT	8-31-79	.4626	11-30-79	.4017	12-	13	7887	59	7547	64	S
3-80	ENDM	SHORT	11-30-79	.4068	12-7-79	.4236	2100-	5	0	1	2165-	5	S
3-80	M M	LONG	12-7-79	.4236	2-19-80	.4086	1875-	49	1987	19	1940-	49	L
3-80	M END	SHORT	2-19-80	.4086	2-29-80	.3980	87-	1	1350	9	1260	10	S
6-80	ENDM	LONG	2-29-80	.4035	4-23-80	.4133	1300-	2	2350	25	1290	37	L
6-80	M END	LONG	4-23-80	.4133	5-30-80	.4474	775-	3	5362	24	4197	28	L
9-80	ENDM	LONG	5-30-80	.4461	7-23-80	.4430	387-	37	2237	7	452-	37	L
9-80	M M	LONG	7-23-80	.4430	8-26-80	.4563	1662-	25	900	4	1727-	25	L
9-80	M END	SHORT	8-26-80	.4563	8-29-80	.4575	287-	3	437	3	85	5	S
12-80	ENDM	LONG	8-29-80	.4591	10-27-80	.4695	550-	16	3512	31	1235	40	L
12-80	M END	SHORT	10-27-80	.4695	11-28-80	.4621	1612-	10	950	23	860	24	S
3-81	ENDM	SHORT	11-28-80	.4696	12-8-80	.4918	2775-	6	225	1	2840-	6	S
3-81	M M	LONG	12-8-80	.4918	2-13-81	.4838	1000-	47	2625	18	1065-	47	L
3-81	M END	SHORT	2-13-81	.4838	2-27-81	.4783	850-	5	925	10	622	11	S
6-81	ENDEND	SHORT	2-27-81	.4878	5-29-81	.4495	1087-	6	5225	61	4722	64	S
9-81	ENDEND	SHORT	5-29-81	.4607	8-31-81	.4324	812-	11	6150	46	3472	66	S
9-81	ENDM	SHORT	8-31-81	.4441	11-3-81	.4467	1737-	10	2075	39	390-	45	S
12-81	M END	LONG	11-3-81	.4467	11-30-81	.4686	1175-	6	2800	19	2672	20	L
12-81	ENDM	LONG	11-30-81	.4747	1-25-82	.4414	4162-	38	150	2	4227-	38	L
3-82	ENDM	SHORT	1-25-82	.4414	2-26-82	.4221	362-	16	2987	16	2347	25	S
3-82	M END	SHORT	2-26-82	.4310	4-26-82	.4245	775-	5	2887	33	747	40	S
6-82	ENDM	LONG	4-26-82	.4245	5-28-82	.4114	1637-	25	1350	10	1702-	25	L
6-82	M END	SHORT	5-28-82	.4114	5-28-82	.3851	287-	1	50	1	65-	2	S
9-82	ENDEND	SHORT	5-28-82	.4188	8-31-82	.3813	887-	2	5350	53	4147	66	S
12-82	ENDM	LONG	8-31-82	.3892	11-16-82	.4018	325-	1	3700	46	922	54	L
12-82	M END	LONG	11-16-82	.3813	11-30-82	.4193	150-	1	2650	10	2497	11	L
3-83	ENDM	LONG	11-30-82	.4047	1-24-83	.4178	1525-	17	4887	28	1760	38	L
3-83	M END	SHORT	1-24-83	.4193	2-28-83	.4346	1800-	51	775	8	122	26	S
6-83	ENDM	LONG	2-28-83	.4202	5-11-83	.4177	2125-	14	587	15	1865-	51	L
6-83	M END	LONG	5-11-83	.4346	5-31-83	.4073	2012-	52	75	14	2177-	15	L
9-83	ENDEND	LONG	5-31-83	.4211	8-31-83	.4312	362-	7	525	16	1815-	66	L
12-83	ENDM	LONG	8-31-83	.4111	11-30-83	.4292	1087-	56	3187	26	2447	63	L
3-84	ENDEND	LONG	11-30-83	.4347	2-29-84	.4304	350-	4	325	21	752-	63	L
3-84	ENDM	LONG	2-29-84	.4332	5-18-84	.4328	875-	2	2912	10	415-	56	L
6-84	M END	SHORT	5-18-84	.4304	5-31-84	.4143	537-	1	175	2	365-	10	S
6-84	ENDM	SHORT	5-31-84	.4389	8-31-84	.4310	250-	39	3912	36	3010	66	S
9-84	M END	SHORT	8-31-84	.4290	9-17-84	.4200	1375-	1	0	1	315-	1	S
12-84	M M	LONG	9-17-84	.4310	11-30-84	.4043	0	39	875	9	1440-	39	L
6-85	ENDEND	SHORT	11-30-84	.4201	2-28-85	.3886	1062-	1	2100	33	1910	64	S
6-85	M END	SHORT	11-30-84	.4200	2-28-85	.3886	312-	6	4675	112	3860	116	S
3-85	ENDEND	SHORT	11-30-84	.4074	2-28-85	.3853	312-	2	3500	58	2697	62	S

TOTALS FOR ALL CONTRACTS OF: JAPANESE YEN

NET PROFIT	=	34673	NUM TRADES	=	54	LARGEST PROFIT	=	7547	AV PROFIT TRADE= 2587 REL PROFIT FACTOR= .90
TOTAL PROFITS	=	72447	NUM WINS	=	28	LARGEST LOSS	=	4227-	AV LOSS TRADE= 1452- AV PROFIT/AV LOSS= 1.78
TOTAL LOSSES	=	37774-	NUM LOSSES	=	26	BEST POSITION	=	11037	AV DAYS IN WIN= 44 MAX WINS IN ROW= 5
PROFIT FACTOR	=	1.91	PERCENT WINS	=	52	WORST POSITION	=	4162-	AV DAYS IN LOSS= 28 MAX LOSSES IN ROW= 5
MAX DRAWDOWN	=	9237-	MARGIN	=	1500	AV BEST POSITION	=	2417	NUM MONTHS= 80 DAY COMMISSION = 65
AV NET PROFIT	=	642	RETURN ON CAP	=	35	AV WORST POSITION	=	1077-	PROFIT/DRAWDOWN= 3.75 NIGHT COMMISSION = 65

68

NYSE COMPOSITE

DELIV	RULE	POSITION	DATE-IN	PRICE-IN	DATE-OUT	PRICE-OUT	MAX-LOSS	DAYS	MAX-GAIN	DAYS	NET-PROFIT	DAYS	
9-82	M END	LONG	8-23-82	66.8000	8-31-82	68.2000	1150-	1	1075	4	635	8	L
12-82	ENDEND	LONG	8-31-82	68.4500	11-30-82	81.6500	625-	2	8000	50	6535	64	L
3-83	ENDEND	LONG	11-30-82	82.3500	2-28-83	86.2000	2225-	11	2925	60	1860	63	L
6-83	ENDEND	LONG	2-28-83	86.8500	5-31-83	94.3000	550-	13	5075	48	3660	65	L
9-83	ENDEND	LONG	5-31-83	95.0500	8-31-83	95.1500	1500-	49	2850	16	15-	66	L
12-83	ENDEND	LONG	8-31-83	95.8000	11-30-83	96.3000	850-	47	2350	27	185	64	L
3-84	ENDM	LONG	11-30-83	97.5000	2-8-84	90.3000	3600-	48	825	27	3665-	48	L
3-84	M END	SHORT	2-8-84	90.3000	2-29-84	90.6000	1325-	13	1200	11	215-	16	S
6-84	ENDEND	SHORT	2-29-84	91.7000	5-31-84	87.0500	1200-	44	2950	63	2260	65	S
9-84	ENDM	SHORT	5-31-84	88.3000	8-3-84	94.7500	3225-	45	1425	38	3290-	45	S
9-84	M END	LONG	8-3-84	94.7500	8-31-84	96.7000	1500-	1	2025	14	910	22	L
12-84	ENDEND	LONG	8-31-84	98.3000	11-30-84	94.9000	2250-	27	1300	34	1765-	64	L
3-85	ENDEND	LONG	11-30-84	96.3500	2-28-85	105.4500	725-	9	5825	51	4485	62	L
6-85	ENDEND	LONG	2-28-85	107.9500	4-26-85	106.3500	1875-	26	1025	1	865-	41	L

TOTALS FOR ALL CONTRACTS OF: NYSE COMPOSITE

NET PROFIT	= 10715	NUM TRADES	= 14	LARGEST PROFIT	= 6535	AV PROFIT TRADE=	2566
TOTAL PROFITS	= 20530	NUM WINS	= 8	LARGEST LOSS	= 3665-	AV LOSS TRADE=	1635-
TOTAL LOSSES	= 9815-	NUM LOSSES	= 6	BEST POSITION	= 8000	AV DAYS IN WIN =	52
PROFIT FACTOR	= 2.09	PERCENT WINS	= 57	WORST POSITION	= 3600-	AV DAYS IN LOSS=	47
MAX DRAWDOWN	= 5765-	MARGIN	= 3500	AV BEST POSITION=	2868	NUM MONTHS =	30
AV NET PROFIT	= 765	RETURN ON CAP=	33	AV WORST POSITION=	1525-	PROFIT/DRAWDOWN=	1.85

REL PROFIT FACTOR= .88
AV PROFIT/AV LOSS= 1.56
MAX WINS IN ROW= 4
MAX LOSSES IN ROW= 2
DAY COMMISSION = 65
NIGHT COMMISSION = 65

69

PLATINUM

DELIV	RULE	POSITION	DATE-IN	PRICE-IN	DATE-OUT	PRICE-OUT	MAX-LOSS	DAYS	MAX-GAIN	DAYS	NET-PROFIT	DAYS
7-78	M END	LONG	1-23-78	218.1000	6-30-78	238.2000	855-	61	2145	89	940	112 L
1-79	ENDM	LONG	6-30-78	244.5000	11-10-78	316.6000	110-	3	7275	85	3540	92 L
1-79	M END	SHORT	11-10-78	316.6000	12-29-78	349.0000	1920-	27	845	5	1685-	35 S
7-79	ENDM	SHORT	12-29-78	357.4000	1-24-79	387.4000	1490-	17	630	2	1555-	17 S
7-79	M	LONG	1-24-79	387.4000	3-6-79	384.0000	370-	2	2330	20	235-	29 L
7-79	M	SHORT	3-6-79	384.0000	4-30-79	408.5000	1225-	39	975	29	1290-	39 S
7-79	M END	LONG	4-30-79	408.5000	6-29-79	423.0000	640-	1	2375	21	660	45 L
1-80	ENDM	LONG	6-29-79	423.9000	7-30-79	388.3000	1780-	20	125	3	1845-	20 L
1-80	M	SHORT	7-30-79	388.3000	8-23-79	417.8000	1475-	19	1315	12	1540-	19 S
1-80	M	LONG	8-23-79	417.8000	10-15-79	500.2000	665-	1	9325	28	4055	37 L
1-80	M	SHORT	10-15-79	500.2000	11-7-79	523.6000	1515-	1	1760	14	1235-	18 S
1-80	M END	LONG	11-7-79	523.6000	12-28-79	692.6000	2305-	7	10320	34	8385	36 L
7-80	ENDM	LONG	1-3-80	767.5000	1-24-80	835.2000	2525-	4	10490	12	3320	15 L
7-80	M	SHORT	1-24-80	835.2000	2-4-80	896.0000	3040-	8	2910	3	3105-	8 S
7-80	M	LONG	2-4-80	896.0000	3-10-80	951.5000	1975-	15	8775	23	2710	25 L
7-80	M	SHORT	3-10-80	951.5000	4-25-80	622.0000	175-	1	21450	15	16410	34 S
7-80	M	LONG	4-25-80	622.0000	5-1-80	546.2000	3790-	5	0	1	3855-	5 L
7-80	M END	SHORT	5-1-80	546.2000	5-30-80	595.3000	2455-	21	960	1	2520-	21 S
1-81	ENDM	LONG	5-30-80	595.3000	6-30-80	676.2000	465-	1	4735	22	3980	23 L
1-81	M	LONG	6-30-80	719.2000	7-15-80	675.0000	2210-	10	2490	5	2275-	10 L
1-81	M	SHORT	7-15-80	675.0000	8-20-80	691.6000	1350-	11	2015	13	895-	27 S
1-81	M	LONG	8-20-80	691.6000	9-29-80	711.0000	880-	4	4565	24	905	28 L
1-81	M END	SHORT	9-29-80	711.0000	12-31-80	578.0000	1500-	1	8850	53	6585	65 S
7-81	ENDM	SHORT	12-31-80	630.0000	3-2-81	539.0000	550-	2	7875	19	4485	26 S
7-81	M	LONG	3-2-81	539.0000	3-16-81	461.4000	3880-	15	0	1	3945-	15 L
7-81	M	SHORT	3-16-81	461.4000	4-9-81	506.7000	2265-	11	635	3	2330-	11 S
7-81	M END	LONG	4-9-81	506.7000	6-30-81	490.8000	795-	19	2890	9	860-	19 L
7-82	ENDM	SHORT	6-30-81	490.8000	8-13-81	404.8000	560-	1	4590	57	4235	58 S
7-82	M	SHORT	8-13-81	438.8000	9-24-81	456.8000	900-	31	1780	23	965-	31 S
7-82	M	LONG	9-24-81	456.8000	12-31-81	437.2000	1440-	9	1110	20	1045-	30 L
7-82	M	SHORT	12-31-81	437.2000	4-5-82	373.2000	540-	13	3585	65	3135	69 S
7-82	M END	SHORT	4-5-82	395.9000	4-30-82	347.0000	355-	2	4570	60	2380	65 S
1-83	ENDM	LONG	4-30-82	347.0000	6-30-82	321.6000	1270-	19	1275	7	1335-	19 L
1-83	M	SHORT	6-30-82	321.6000	7-9-82	276.7000	1270-	1	4180	36	2180	44 S
1-83	M	SHORT	7-9-82	296.4000	8-9-82	310.2000	690-	6	1245	4	755-	6 S
1-83	M	SHORT	8-9-82	310.2000	8-19-82	273.3000	1845-	22	840	11	1910	22 S
1-83	M	LONG	8-19-82	273.3000	9-20-82	333.6000	3015-	9	440	3	3080	9 L
1-83	M	LONG	9-20-82	333.6000	10-11-82	300.4000	1660-	22	3895	13	1725-	22 L
1-83	M	LONG	10-11-82	300.4000	12-30-82	351.3000	2545-	16	1135	11	2610	16 L
1-83	M END	LONG	12-30-82	351.3000	2-23-83	383.1000	1815-	23	2170	55	1525	57 L
1-84	ENDM	LONG	12-30-82	400.1000	2-22-83	443.6000	0	1	5245	22	2110	37 L
1-84	M	SHORT	2-22-83	482.5000	2-22-83	458.1000	0	1	1220	1	1155	1 S
1-84	M	LONG	2-22-83	458.1000	2-23-83	445.8000	615-	3	895	2	680-	3 L
7-83	M	SHORT	2-25-83	443.6000	4-14-83	432.8000	895-	2	3070	21	475	37 S
1-84	M	SHORT	2-23-83	445.8000	4-18-83	456.1000	1085-	1	2490	3	580-	36 S
1-84	M	LONG	4-18-83	456.1000	6-1-83	432.7000	1170-	32	1620	31	1235-	32 L
1-84	M END	SHORT	6-1-83	432.7000	12-30-83	390.5000	1715-	39	2885	110	2045	149 S

TOTALS FOR ALL CONTRACTS OF: PLATINUM

NET PROFIT = 30125	NUM TRADES = 47	LARGEST PROFIT = 16410	AV PROFIT TRADE= 3581	REL PROFIT FACTOR= 2.90
TOTAL PROFITS = 75215	NUM WINS = 26	LARGEST LOSS = 3945-	AV LOSS TRADE= 1734-	AV PROFIT/AV LOSS= 2.06
TOTAL LOSSES = 45090-	NUM LOSSES = 21	BEST POSITION = 21450	AV DAYS IN WIN= 50	MAX WINS IN ROW= 3
PROFIT FACTOR = 1.66	PERCENT WINS = 55	WORST POSITION = 3880-	AV DAYS IN LOSS= 20	MAX LOSSES IN ROW= 5
MAX DRAWDOWN = 12080-	MARGIN = 1000	AV BEST POSITION = 4020	NUM MONTHS= 65	DAY COMMISSION = 65
AV NET PROFIT = 640	RETURN ON CAP = 37	AV WORST POSITION= 914-	PROFIT/DRAWDOWN= 2.98	NIGHT COMMISSION = 65

PORK BELLIES

DELIV	RULE	POSITION	DATE-IN	PRICE-IN	DATE-OUT	PRICE-OUT	MAX-LOSS	DAYS	MAX-GAIN	DAYS	NET-PROFIT	DAYS	
2-78	M END	LONG	1-4-78	59.6405	1-31-78	63.6500	662-	15	1731	19	1378	21	L
7-78	ENDM	LONG	1-20-78	61.5500	3-20-78	76.4849	0	1	8154	29	5311	33	L
7-78	M MO	SHORT	3-20-78	76.4849	3-28-78	84.0000	2705-	6	264	1	2770-	6	S
7-78	MO M	LONG	3-28-78	84.0000	4-10-78	77.4182	2369-	10	630	2	2434-	10	L
7-78	M END	SHORT	4-10-78	77.4182	6-30-78	50.0500	749-	1	11454	57	9787	60	S
2-79	ENDMO	SHORT	6-30-78	54.4000	7-27-78	58.8000	1672-	18	988	12	1737-	18	S
2-79	MO M	LONG	7-27-78	58.8000	9-13-78	57.1608	1330-	13	1862	8	687-	34	L
2-79	M MO	SHORT	9-13-78	57.1608	9-19-78	62.9500	2199-	5	4	1	2264-	5	S
2-79	MO M	LONG	9-19-78	62.9500	10-20-78	67.6843	684-	2	4085	14	1734	24	L
2-79	M MO	SHORT	10-20-78	67.6843	11-22-78	67.9313	252-	1	1970	10	158-	23	S
2-79	M M	LONG	11-22-78	67.9313	12-11-78	63.6768	1616-	12	672	7	1681-	12	L
2-79	M M	SHORT	12-11-78	63.6768	1-24-79	61.2123	445-	1	3240	12	871	31	S
2-79	M END	LONG	1-24-79	61.2123	1-31-79	63.7000	365-	1	1201	4	880	7	L
7-79	ENDM	LONG	1-31-79	63.5000	3-6-79	64.1245	418-	1	2755	14	172	23	L
7-79	M M	SHORT	3-6-79	64.1245	4-27-79	60.8877	465-	1	4322	22	1164	38	S
7-79	M M	LONG	4-27-79	60.8877	5-4-79	56.5655	1642-	6	460	1	1707-	6	L
7-79	M END	SHORT	5-4-79	56.5655	6-29-79	35.2750	716-	1	8090	40	8025	41	S
2-80	ENDM	SHORT	6-29-79	42.5750	8-13-79	42.2696	2099-	6	2042	23	51	30	S
2-80	M M	LONG	8-13-79	42.2696	9-25-79	43.6078	976-	3	3602	23	443	31	L
2-80	M M	SHORT	9-25-79	43.6078	10-23-79	46.1143	1574-	6	1351	15	1017-	21	S
2-80	M M	LONG	10-23-79	46.1143	11-29-79	49.5982	708-	2	3756	22	1258	27	L
2-80	M END	SHORT	11-29-79	49.5982	1-31-80	40.5000	1254-	13	4017	36	3392	44	S
7-80	ENDM	SHORT	1-31-80	45.2753	3-3-80	45.4886	370-	4	1605	16	146-	21	S
7-80	M MO	LONG	3-3-80	45.4886	3-25-80	40.8000	1781-	17	859	13	1846-	17	L
7-80	MO M	SHORT	3-25-80	40.8000	6-25-80	34.9500	361-	2	5130	52	2158	65	S
7-80	MO END	LONG	6-25-80	34.9500	6-30-80	38.8000	256-	1	1539	4	1398	5	L
2-81	ENDM	LONG	6-30-80	53.0250	8-25-80	58.3922	161-	1	4816	30	1974	39	L
2-81	M M	SHORT	8-25-80	58.3922	9-4-80	63.1367	1802-	8	510	4	1867-	8	S
2-81	M M	LONG	9-4-80	63.1367	9-26-80	64.9411	355-	13	3406	13	620	17	L
2-81	M MO	SHORT	9-26-80	64.9411	10-10-80	69.5262	1742-	11	1108	6	1807-	11	S
2-81	MO M	LONG	10-10-80	69.5262	11-10-80	66.9500	978-	21	1510	10	1043-	21	L
2-81	M M	SHORT	11-10-80	66.9500	11-20-80	72.3218	2041-	9	589	3	2106-	9	S
2-81	M MO	LONG	11-20-80	72.3218	12-5-80	67.1558	1963-	11	827	7	2028-	11	L
2-81	MO M	SHORT	12-5-80	67.1558	1-30-81	54.3500	548-	6	6291	30	4801	39	S
7-81	M END	SHORT	1-30-81	59.7250	2-9-81	61.2169	566-	12	1510	4	631-	6	S
7-81	ENDM	LONG	2-9-81	61.2169	2-25-81	58.1193	1177-	7	1342	7	1242-	12	L
7-81	M M	SHORT	2-25-81	58.1193	3-26-81	52.4500	410-	1	5507	14	2089	22	S
7-81	M M	LONG	3-26-81	52.4500	4-24-81	55.9000	247-	1	3800	14	1246	21	L
7-81	M M	SHORT	4-24-81	55.9000	5-26-81	54.3500	1083-	3	4294	17	524	21	S
7-81	M M	LONG	5-26-81	54.3500	6-17-81	52.7000	950-	7	1605	11	692-	17	L
7-81	M END	SHORT	6-17-81	52.7000	6-30-81	45.5000	1007-	3	2736	10	2671	11	S
2-82	ENDM	SHORT	6-30-81	63.0000	8-6-81	66.5766	2014-	4	1045	16	1424-	26	S
2-82	M M	LONG	8-6-81	66.5766	8-27-81	63.9839	985-	11	1395	11	1050-	16	L
2-82	M M	SHORT	8-27-81	63.9839	9-8-81	70.0900	2320-	16	145	4	2385-	8	S
2-82	M M	LONG	9-8-81	70.0900	9-23-81	64.5000	2124-	12	706	3	2189-	12	L
2-82	M M	SHORT	9-23-81	64.5000	10-19-81	66.6463	815-	19	1064	4	880-	19	S
2-82	M M	LONG	10-19-81	66.6463	11-17-81	65.7825	758-	16	1578	16	393-	21	L
2-82	M END	SHORT	11-17-81	65.7825	12-29-81	60.9500	652-	1	5731	23	1771	29	S
7-82	M MO	LONG	12-29-81	60.9500	1-29-82	74.4750	798-	10	4123	23	4058	24	L
7-82	MO END	LONG	1-29-82	74.4750	2-9-82	69.0422	2064-	7	427	4	2129-	7	L
7-82	ENDM	SHORT	2-9-82	69.0422	2-23-82	73.4323	1668-	10	586	3	1733-	10	S
7-82	M M	LONG	2-23-82	73.4323	5-20-82	84.0892	1370-	5	6295	56	3984	62	L
2-83	M END	SHORT	5-20-82	84.0892	6-30-82	73.6750	1106-	10	5999	21	3483	30	S
2-83	ENDM	SHORT	6-30-82	73.6750	7-22-82	76.7000	1149-	15	1377	5	1214-	15	S
2-83	MO M	LONG	7-22-82	76.7000	8-11-82	73.6366	1164-	15	1045	8	1229-	15	L

71

PORK BELLIES

DELIV	RULE	POSITION	DATE-IN	PRICE-IN	DATE-OUT	PRICE-OUT	MAX-LOSS	DAYS	MAX-GAIN	DAYS	NET-PROFIT	DAYS	
2-83	M MO	SHORT	8-11-82	73.6366	8-13-82	79.4000	2190-	3	80	1	2255-	3	S
2-83	MO M	LONG	8-13-82	79.4000	9-14-82	83.6401	912-	3	4408	19	1546	22	L
2-83	M MO	SHORT	9-14-82	83.6401	9-27-82	88.9000	1998-	10	1079	6	2063-	10	S
2-83	MO M	LONG	9-27-82	88.9000	10-1-82	82.3292	2496-	5	0	1	2561-	5	L
2-83	M M	SHORT	10-1-82	82.3292	11-12-82	82.2557	919-	13	2367	23	37-	31	S
2-83	M MO	LONG	11-12-82	82.2557	11-26-82	78.4416	1449-	10	1346	6	1514-	10	L
2-83	M MO	SHORT	11-26-82	78.4416	1-14-83	86.3250	2995-	35	918	8	3060-	35	S
2-83	MO M	LONG	1-14-83	86.3250	1-28-83	81.6922	1760-	11	750	2	1825-	11	L
2-83	M END	SHORT	1-28-83	81.6922	1-31-83	80.4750	934-	1	681	2	397	3	S
7-83	END END	SHORT	1-31-83	78.8250	6-30-83	60.8500	769-	2	8189	96	6765	102	S
2-83	ENDMO	SHORT	6-30-83	55.9000	7-21-83	59.0250	1187-	14	836	2	1252-	14	S
2-84	MO MO	LONG	7-21-83	59.0250	9-21-83	59.2500	408-	1	4132	19	20	44	L
2-84	MO M	SHORT	9-21-83	59.2500	10-17-83	60.9200	634-	19	1159	14	699	19	S
2-84	M M	LONG	10-17-83	60.9200	1-3-84	60.7056	1109-	34	1911	48	146-	53	L
2-84	M M	SHORT	1-3-84	60.7056	1-13-84	66.4759	2192-	9	306	2	2257-	9	S
2-84	M END	LONG	1-13-84	66.4759	1-31-84	65.5000	551-	1	1187	4	435-	14	L
7-84	ENDMO	LONG	1-31-84	68.4750	2-13-84	65.1500	1263-	9	256	2	1328-	9	L
7-84	MO M	SHORT	2-13-84	65.1500	3-9-84	66.6529	571-	19	1786	12	636-	19	S
7-84	M LONG	LONG	3-9-84	66.6529	4-18-84	68.1000	1008-	5	2563	20	484	29	L
7-84	MO M	SHORT	4-18-84	68.1000	6-12-84	68.9294	1007-	13	2014	28	380-	38	S
7-84	M MO	LONG	6-12-84	68.9294	6-26-84	66.3500	980-	11	1166	8	1045-	11	L
7-84	MO END	SHORT	6-26-84	66.3500	6-29-84	62.7000	19-	1	1691	3	1322	5	S
2-85	ENDM	SHORT	6-29-84	77.0250	10-4-84	65.6429	142-	1	6127	59	4260	67	S
2-85	M LONG	LONG	10-4-84	65.6429	10-19-84	62.0139	1379-	12	439	7	1444-	12	L
2-85	M M	SHORT	10-19-84	62.0139	10-31-84	67.0023	1895-	9	128	1	1960-	9	S
2-85	M LONG	LONG	10-31-84	67.0023	12-10-84	70.5511	665-	1	3324	22	1283	28	L
2-85	MO M	SHORT	12-10-84	70.5511	12-26-84	77.5800	2670-	12	266	2	2735-	12	S
2-85	MO M	LONG	12-26-84	77.5800	1-16-85	71.9852	2126-	15	235	1	2191-	15	L
2-85	M END	SHORT	1-16-85	71.9852	1-31-85	71.2500	537-	5	1324	5	214	13	S
7-85	ENDM	SHORT	1-31-85	73.2250	3-6-85	73.4746	712-	2	2137	16	159-	23	S
7-85	M M	LONG	3-6-85	73.4746	4-1-85	70.8616	1149-	8	636	4	1057-	19	L
7-85	M END	SHORT	4-1-85	70.8616	4-26-85	65.8750	565-	1	2531	11	1829	20	S

TOTALS FOR ALL CONTRACTS OF: PORK BELLIES

NET PROFIT = 9835	NUM TRADES = 87	LARGEST PROFIT = 9787	AV PROFIT TRADE= 2315	REL PROFIT FACTOR= 1.65
TOTAL PROFITS = 83363	NUM WINS = 36	LARGEST LOSS = 3060-	AV LOSS TRADE= 1441-	AV PROFIT/AV LOSS= 1.60
TOTAL LOSSES = 73528-	NUM LOSSES = 51	BEST POSITION = 11454	AV DAYS IN WIN = 31	MAX WINS IN ROW= 4
PROFIT FACTOR = 1.13	PERCENT WINS = 41	WORST POSITION = 2995-	AV DAYS IN LOSS= 16	MAX LOSSES IN ROW= 6
MAX DRAWDOWN = 17191-	MARGIN = 1500	AV BEST POSITION= 2398	NUM MONTHS = 87	DAY COMMISSION = 65
AV NET PROFIT = 113	RETURN ON CAP= 6	AV WORST POSITION= 1089-	PROFIT/DRAWDOWN= .57	NIGHT COMMISSION = 65

72

COMEX SILVER

REL PROFIT FACTOR= 3.44
AV PROFIT/AV LOSS= 5.74
MAX WINS IN ROW= 6
MAX LOSSES IN ROW= 3
DAY COMMISSION = 65
NIGHT COMMISSION = 65

DELIV	RULE	POSITION	DATE-IN	PRICE-IN	DATE-OUT	PRICE-OUT	MAX-LOSS	DAYS	MAX-GAIN	DAYS	NET-PROFIT	DAYS	S/L
3-78	ENDEND	SHORT	12-30-77	485.0000	2-28-78	496.0000	1175-	15	150	26	615-	39	S
9-78	ENDEND	SHORT	2-28-78	517.5000	8-31-78	548.0000	2875-	10	975	39	1590-	130	S
3-79	ENDM	SHORT	8-31-78	572.0000	10-30-78	650.0000	3900-	41	475	5	3965-	41	S
3-79	M END	LONG	10-30-78	650.0000	2-28-79	771.0000	3625-	9	7700	78	5985	84	L
9-79	ENDEND	LONG	2-28-79	801.0000	8-31-79	1061.5000	3425-	8	13450	129	12960	130	L
3-80	ENDM	LONG	8-31-79	1104.5000	1-24-80	3850.0000	0	1	152275	96	137210	99	L
3-80	M	SHORT	1-24-80	3850.0000	2-7-80	3675.0000	10000-	1	23750	8	8685	11	S
3-80	M	LONG	2-7-80	3675.0000	2-14-80	3660.0000	750-	6	14750	4	815-	6	S
3-80	M	SHORT	2-14-80	3660.0000	2-28-80	3520.0000	7000-	1	19500	7	6935	10	S
3-80	M END	LONG	2-28-80	3520.0000	2-29-80	3530.0000	4500-	2	2500	1	435	3	L
9-80	ENDM	LONG	2-29-80	3784.0000	3-7-80	3647.0000	6850-	5	5800	3	6915-	5	L
9-80	M	LONG	3-7-80	3417.0000	5-30-80	1417.0000	0	1	126750	54	111435	59	S
9-80	M END	SHORT	5-30-80	1417.0000	7-15-80	1555.0000	3600-	1	18900	7	6835	32	S
3-81	ENDM	SHORT	7-15-80	1555.0000	8-29-80	1630.0000	6500-	9	1250	4	3815-	35	S
3-81	M	LONG	8-29-80	1744.0000	9-4-80	1787.5000	2175-	3	650	3	2240-	3	L
3-81	ENDM	SHORT	9-4-80	1787.5000	9-29-80	2252.0000	1175-	1	35575	14	23160	18	S
9-81	M	LONG	9-29-80	2252.0000	2-27-81	1217.5000	3400-	10	52000	104	51660	105	S
3-81	M	SHORT	2-27-81	1320.0000	3-18-81	1393.0000	3650-	13	4500	4	3715-	13	S
3-81	M	LONG	3-18-81	1393.0000	3-31-81	1266.0000	6350-	10	1300	4	6415-	10	L
3-81	M	SHORT	3-31-81	1266.0000	8-18-81	950.0000	2300-	5	21600	87	15735	98	S
8-81	M END	SHORT	8-18-81	950.0000	8-18-81	929.5000	4100-	8	1400	2	1090-	11	L
3-82	ENDM	LONG	8-18-81	1013.2000	9-24-81	1018.0000	1410-	1	1090	9	175	11	S
9-82	M END	SHORT	9-24-81	1018.0000	2-26-82	774.3000	1300-	15	10690	108	12120	109	L
3-82	ENDM	LONG	2-26-82	833.0000	7-9-82	651.0000	950-	24	12250	79	9035	92	S
3-83	M	SHORT	7-9-82	651.0000	8-31-82	787.0000	1850-	11	17050	35	6735	39	L
3-83	M	LONG	8-31-82	826.3000	9-27-82	859.0000	1715-	1	9850	5	1570	18	S
3-83	M	SHORT	9-27-82	859.0000	10-11-82	984.5000	6275-	17	9835	6	6340-	11	S
3-83	M END	LONG	10-11-82	984.5000	11-11-82	973.8000	1725-	1	1650	17	600-	23	L
3-83	M	SHORT	11-11-82	973.8000	12-2-82	1066.0000	4610-	9	6825	1	4675-	15	S
9-83	ENDM	LONG	12-2-82	1066.0000	2-23-83	1356.0000	2200-	10	2840	9	14435	57	L
9-83	M	SHORT	2-23-83	1356.0000	2-28-83	1030.0000	1400-	2	21350	52	16235	5	S
3-84	ENDM	LONG	2-28-83	1232.6000	4-14-83	1229.0000	0	1	16800	4	115	32	S
3-84	M	SHORT	4-14-83	1229.0000	6-1-83	1280.8000	1450-	25	9380	5	2525	34	L
3-84	M END	LONG	6-1-83	1280.8000	8-31-83	1210.0000	960-	5	8950	25	3475	66	S
3-84	M	SHORT	8-31-83	1274.8000	11-29-83	966.0000	1660-	3	7990	1	15375	62	S
9-84	M	LONG	11-29-83	966.0000	12-16-83	877.0000	4450-	14	21140	55	4515-	14	L
9-84	M END	SHORT	12-16-83	877.0000	2-1-84	886.0000	2150-	10	3100	8	515-	32	S
3-85	M	LONG	2-1-84	886.0000	2-29-84	966.0000	1400-	7	4700	15	3935	21	L
9-84	ENDM	LONG	2-29-84	1015.5000	5-7-84	892.3000	6160-	47	5250	18	6225-	47	S
9-84	M END	SHORT	5-7-84	892.3000	8-31-84	745.2000	4460-	19	2525	3	7290	84	S
3-85	ENDEND	SHORT	8-31-84	788.7000	2-28-85	562.5000	1115-	15	10365	58	11245	124	S

TOTALS FOR ALL CONTRACTS OF: COMEX SILVER

NET PROFIT	= 431255	NUM TRADES	= 41	LARGEST PROFIT	= 137210	AV PROFIT TRADE	= 19412
TOTAL PROFITS	= 485300	NUM WINS	= 25	LARGEST LOSS	= 6915-	AV LOSS TRADE	= 3377-
TOTAL LOSSES	= 54045-	NUM LOSSES	= 16	BEST POSITION	= 152275	AV DAYS IN WIN	= 56
PROFIT FACTOR	= 8.97	PERCENT WINS	= 61	WORST POSITION	= 10000-	AV DAYS IN LOSS	= 27
MAX DRAWDOWN	= 11615-	MARGIN	= 4000	AV BEST POSITION	= 18513	NUM MONTHS	= 80
AV NET PROFIT	= 10518	RETURN ON CAP	= 253	AV WORST POSITION	= 1570-	PROFIT/DRAWDOWN	= 37.12

73

SOYBEANS

DELIV	RULE	POSITION	DATE-IN	PRICE-IN	DATE-OUT	PRICE-OUT	MAX-LOSS	DAYS	MAX-GAIN	DAYS	NET-PROFIT	DAYS	
7-78	M M	SHORT	1-17-78	575.5000	3-1-78	616.5000	2050-	31	225	1	2115-	31	S
7-78	M M	LONG	3-1-78	616.5000	6-14-78	665.0000	925-	1	7075	63	2360	74	L
7-78	M END	SHORT	6-14-78	665.0000	6-30-78	685.0000	1700-	10	450	1	1065-	14	S
11-78	M M	SHORT	6-30-78	630.5000	8-15-78	636.0000	275-	31	2250	26	340-	31	S
11-78	M M	LONG	8-15-78	636.0000	10-31-78	707.2500	700-	1	4750	54	3497	56	L
11-78	M END	LONG	10-31-78	736.5000	6-29-79	741.5000	3175-	11	6125	161	185	166	L
7-79	M END	SHORT	6-29-79	741.5000	6-29-79	741.5000	750-	1	0	1	65-	2	S
11-79	ENDEND	SHORT	6-29-79	739.0000	10-31-79	645.0000	3150-	5	5700	84	4635	87	S
11-79	ENDM	SHORT	10-31-79	725.2500	6-30-80	671.0000	1487-	15	6512	103	2647	164	S
7-80	M END	LONG	6-30-80	671.0000	6-30-80	671.0000	775-	1	37	1	65-	2	L
11-80	ENDM	LONG	6-30-80	704.0000	9-26-80	806.0000	275-	1	8800	58	5035	62	L
11-80	M M	SHORT	9-26-80	806.0000	10-22-80	896.5000	4525-	19	1100	2	4590-	19	S
11-80	M M	LONG	10-22-80	896.5000	10-31-80	946.5000	675-	4	1325	7	90-	9	L
7-81	M END	LONG	10-31-80	973.2500	12-3-80	946.5000	1337-	21	2537	18	1402-	21	L
7-81	ENDM	SHORT	12-3-80	946.5000	4-7-81	833.0000	1325-	1	10125	62	5610	86	S
7-81	M M	LONG	4-7-81	833.0000	5-12-81	760.2500	3637-	25	300	1	3702-	25	L
7-81	M END	SHORT	5-12-81	760.2500	6-30-81	686.5000	762-	7	4362	34	3622	36	S
11-81	ENDM	LONG	6-30-81	731.0000	7-10-81	787.0000	2800-	7	150	3	2865-	7	L
11-81	M M	LONG	7-10-81	787.0000	8-13-81	694.5000	4925-	25	550	2	4690-	25	S
11-81	M END	SHORT	8-13-81	694.5000	10-30-81	651.5000	925-	6	2900	32	2085	57	S
7-82	M M	SHORT	10-30-81	729.5000	4-5-82	671.5000	375-	1	5725	92	2835	107	S
7-82	M M	LONG	4-5-82	671.5000	5-28-82	635.7500	1787-	39	625	19	1852-	39	L
7-82	M END	SHORT	5-28-82	635.7500	6-30-82	610.2500	512-	10	1287	23	1210	24	S
11-82	ENDEND	SHORT	6-30-82	624.5000	10-29-82	533.2500	400-	9	5325	66	4497	86	S
11-82	ENDM	SHORT	10-29-82	575.2500	3-23-83	650.7500	3775-	98	0	98	3840-	98	S
7-83	M M	LONG	3-23-83	650.7500	6-29-83	576.0000	3737-	69	1112	13	3802-	69	L
7-83	M END	SHORT	6-29-83	576.0000	6-30-83	606.0000	1500-	2	25	1	1565-	3	S
11-83	M M	SHORT	6-30-83	628.2500	7-11-83	667.0000	1962-	6	212	2	2027-	6	L
11-83	M M	LONG	7-11-83	667.5000	9-15-83	857.5000	625-	1	15050	46	9435	48	L
11-83	M END	SHORT	9-15-83	857.5000	10-31-83	812.0000	4975-	6	3075	31	2210	34	S
7-84	M END	SHORT	10-31-83	846.0000	12-27-83	854.5000	2700-	7	3200	24	490-	39	S
7-84	M M	LONG	12-27-83	854.5000	1-17-84	765.7500	4437-	15	25	1	4502-	15	L
7-84	M M	SHORT	1-17-84	765.7500	3-5-84	795.5000	1487-	34	2287	21	1552-	34	S
7-84	M M	LONG	3-5-84	795.5000	6-1-84	826.5000	1025-	33	5175	55	1485	63	L
11-84	M END	SHORT	6-1-84	826.5000	6-29-84	747.7500	1275-	1	5525	20	3872	22	S
11-84	M END	LONG	6-29-84	728.0000	10-15-84	632.7500	200-	12	7975	58	4697	74	L
11-84	M M	LONG	10-15-84	632.7500	10-31-84	619.0000	1112-	12	462	6	752-	14	L
7-85	M END	LONG	10-31-84	667.5000	1-4-85	595.2500	3612-	44	850	1	3677-	44	L
7-85	M END	SHORT	1-4-85	595.2500	4-26-85	604.2500	1887-	17	725	41	515-	80	S

TOTALS FOR ALL CONTRACTS OF: SOYBEANS

NET PROFIT = 14354	NUM TRADES = 39	LARGEST PROFIT = 9435	AV PROFIT TRADE = 3524	REL PROFIT FACTOR = .73
TOTAL PROFITS = 59917	NUM WINS = 17	LARGEST LOSS = 4690-	AV LOSS TRADE = 2071-	AV PROFIT/AV LOSS = 1.70
TOTAL LOSSES = 45563-	NUM LOSSES = 22	BEST POSITION = 15050	AV DAYS IN WIN = 73	MAX WINS IN ROW = 3
PROFIT FACTOR = 1.31	PERCENT WINS = 44	WORST POSITION = 4975-	AV DAYS IN LOSS = 29	MAX LOSSES IN ROW = 4
MAX DRAWDOWN = 11234-	MARGIN = 3500	AV BEST POSITION = 3893	NUM MONTHS = 84	DAY COMMISSION = 65
AV NET PROFI = 368	RETURN ON CAP = 10	AV WORST POSITION = 1150-	PROFIT/DRAWDOWN = 1.27	NIGHT COMMISSION = 65

SOYBEAN MEAL

DELIV	RULE	POSITION	DATE-IN	PRICE-IN	DATE-OUT	PRICE-OUT	MAX-LOSS	DAYS	MAX-GAIN	DAYS	NET-PROFIT	DAYS	
7-78	M	SHORT	1-17-78	157.8000	3-8-78	173.1000	1530-	36	260	18	1595-	36	S
7-78	M END	LONG	3-8-78	173.1000	6-30-78	174.8000	580-	69	2340	13	105	82	L
12-78	ENDEND	LONG	6-30-78	171.1000	11-30-78	185.1000	1260-	26	3190	84	1335	106	L
7-79	ENDM	LONG	11-30-78	187.1000	6-29-79	199.2000	310-	2	4940	141	1145	146	L
7-79	M END	SHORT	6-29-79	199.2000	6-29-79	195.9000	610-	1	110	1	65-	2	S
12-79	ENDM	SHORT	6-29-79	198.5000	11-15-79	196.8000	1900-	5	2150	84	195	97	S
12-79	M END	LONG	11-15-79	195.9000	11-30-79	202.0000	440-	10	360	6	25	12	L
7-80	ENDM	LONG	11-30-79	202.0000	1-9-80	186.3000	1570-	23	110	1	1635-	23	L
7-80	M END	SHORT	1-9-80	186.3000	6-30-80	179.4000	1670-	7	2080	60	625	122	S
12-80	ENDM	SHORT	6-30-80	193.7000	7-2-80	203.2000	950-	2	40	1	1015-	2	S
12-80	M END	LONG	7-2-80	203.2000	11-28-80	269.3000	570-	1	8630	88	6545	105	L
7-81	ENDM	LONG	11-28-80	299.2000	12-5-80	273.5000	2570-	5	130	1	2635-	5	L
7-81	M	SHORT	12-5-80	273.5000	4-7-81	238.3000	450-	55	6170	60	3455	84	S
7-81	M END	LONG	4-7-81	238.3000	6-24-81	198.9000	3940-	1	240	3	4005-	55	L
12-81	ENDEND	SHORT	6-24-81	198.9000	6-30-81	195.9000	330-	5	770	4	235	6	S
12-81	ENDM	SHORT	6-30-81	211.2000	11-30-81	187.4000	1680-	4	2850	103	2315	107	S
12-82	M END	SHORT	11-30-81	200.9000	6-30-82	178.3000	510-	8	2270	147	2195	148	S
12-82	ENDM	LONG	6-30-82	184.4000	11-5-82	172.5000	260-	1	3340	66	1125	89	L
7-83	M END	LONG	11-5-82	172.5000	11-30-82	175.4000	470-	4	720	11	225	18	L
7-83	ENDM	LONG	11-30-82	179.2000	2-28-83	174.6000	700-	18	1030	42	525-	61	L
12-83	M END	SHORT	2-28-83	174.6000	3-23-83	195.6000	2100-	69	60	1	2165-	18	S
12-83	ENDM	LONG	3-23-83	195.6000	6-30-83	176.9000	2790-	2	220	5	1935-	71	L
7-84	M END	LONG	6-30-83	185.2000	8-30-83	234.3000	270-	10	8330	32	4845	42	L
7-84	ENDM	SHORT	8-30-83	234.3000	11-30-83	223.2000	2360-	18	1830	59	1045	66	S
12-84	M END	SHORT	11-30-83	225.5000	3-2-84	210.4000	350-	51	3200	51	1445	64	L
7-84	M	LONG	3-2-84	210.4000	4-11-84	199.1000	1130-	29	260	1	1195-	29	L
7-84	M END	SHORT	4-11-84	199.1000	6-29-84	177.0000	790-	1	2700	54	2145	57	S
12-84	ENDEND	SHORT	6-29-84	190.2000	11-30-84	150.2000	130-	1	4300	68	3935	108	S
7-85	ENDEND	SHORT	11-30-84	169.7000	4-26-85	129.2000	80-	2	4070	101	3985	102	S

TOTALS FOR ALL CONTRACTS OF: SOYBEAN MEAL

NET PROFIT = 20155	NUM TRADES = 29	LARGEST PROFIT = 6545	AV PROFIT TRADE= 1943	REL PROFIT FACTOR= .74	
TOTAL PROFITS = 36925	NUM WINS = 19	LARGEST LOSS = 4005-	AV LOSS TRADE= 1677-	AV PROFIT/AV LOSS= 1.15	
TOTAL LOSSES = 16770-	NUM LOSSES = 10	BEST POSITION = 8630	AV DAYS IN WIN= 82	MAX WINS IN ROW= 5	
PROFIT FACTOR = 2.20	PERCENT WINS = 66	WORST POSITION = 3940-	AV DAYS IN LOSS= 30	MAX LOSSES IN ROW= 3	
MAX DRAWDOWN = 4625-	MARGIN = 2000	AV BEST POSITION= 2498	NUM MONTHS = 82	DAY COMMISSION = 65	
AV NET PROFIT = 695	RETURN ON CAP= 28	AV WORST POSITION= 913-	PROFIT/DRAWDOWN= 4.35	NIGHT COMMISSION= 65	

75

WORLD SUGAR

DELIV	RULE	POSITION	DATE-IN	PRICE-IN	DATE-OUT	PRICE-OUT	MAX-LOSS	DAYS	MAX-GAIN	DAYS	NET-PROFIT	DAYS
9-78	H END	SHORT	2- 8-78	9.6124	7-31-78	6.3500	75-	3	4090	115	3588	120 S
3-79	ENDM	SHORT	7-31-78	6.9000	8- 7-78	7.7238	922-	5	11	1	987-	5 S
3-79	H	LONG	8- 7-78	7.7238	10-17-78	8.7509	396-	2	2381	47	1085	50 L
3-79	H	SHORT	10-17-78	8.7509	10-26-78	9.7043	1067-	8	57	3	1132-	8 S
3-79	H	LONG	10-26-78	9.7043	11- 8-78	8.7332	1087-	9	196	3	1152-	9 L
3-79	H END	SHORT	11- 8-78	8.7332	1-31-79	8.2200	343-	1	921	54	509	59 S
9-79	H	SHORT	1-31-79	9.0000	6- 4-79	8.8851	571-	13	940	82	63	85 S
9-79	H	LONG	6- 4-79	8.8851	7-23-79	8.4379	655-	11	319	26	565-	35 L
9-79	H END	SHORT	7-23-79	8.4379	7-31-79	8.4700	226-	1	210	2	100-	8 S
3-80	H	SHORT	7-31-79	10.0700	9- 5-79	11.0009	1042-	25	145	5	1107-	25 S
3-80	H	LONG	9- 5-79	11.0009	12-10-79	15.5036	561-	13	6976	63	4978	68 L
3-80	H	SHORT	12-10-79	15.5036	12-18-79	16.8065	1459-	7	732	4	1524-	7 S
3-80	H	LONG	12-18-79	16.8065	1- 2-80	15.6832	1258-	9	664	6	1323-	9 L
3-80	H	SHORT	1- 2-80	15.6832	1-11-80	16.6601	1150-	8	653	4	1159-	8 S
3-80	H	LONG	1-11-80	16.6601	1-28-80	18.6880	627-	2	4726	10	2206	12 L
3-80	H	SHORT	1-28-80	18.6880	1-31-80	20.2365	1734-	2	826	1	1799-	2 S
3-80	H END	LONG	1-29-80	20.2365	2-26-80	22.0100	1664-	1	2031	3	1921	4 L
9-80	H MO	LONG	1-31-80	22.2400	2-27-80	24.9996	100-	1	6843	10	3025	16 L
9-80	H MO	SHORT	2-26-80	24.9996	2-28-80	26.9000	2128-	2	55	1	2193-	2 S
9-80	H MO	LONG	2-27-80	26.9000	2-28-80	24.8032	2348-	2	78	1	2413-	2 L
9-80	H MO	SHORT	2-28-80	24.8032	2-29-80	26.9000	2348-	2	3	1	2413-	2 S
9-80	H MO	LONG	2-29-80	26.9000	3- 7-80	26.6000	336-	6	2340	3	401-	6 L
9-80	H	SHORT	3- 7-80	26.6000	3-24-80	23.2891	224-	1	7336	4	3643	12 S
9-80	H	LONG	3-24-80	23.2891	3-25-80	21.3807	2137-	2	684	8	2202-	2 L
9-80	H	SHORT	3-25-80	21.3807	4- 3-80	22.0953	1141-	2	1546	1	865-	8 S
9-80	H	LONG	4- 3-80	22.0953	5-21-80	32.7540	890-	1	15181	5	11872	34 L
9-80	H MO	SHORT	5-21-80	32.7540	5-27-80	35.9900	3624-	4	71	32	3689-	4 S
9-80	H MO	LONG	5-27-80	35.9900	6- 3-80	33.9100	2329-	6	2251	1	2394-	6 L
9-80	H	SHORT	6- 3-80	33.9100	6-12-80	34.5400	1220-	2	3819	4	770-	8 S
9-80	H	LONG	6-12-80	34.5400	6-24-80	34.4469	716-	4	2172	6	169-	9 L
9-80	H	SHORT	6-24-80	34.4469	7-14-80	29.2971	1403-	2	10020	2	5702	14 S
9-80	H	LONG	7-14-80	29.2971	7-15-80	27.4597	2057-	1	48	13	2122-	2 L
9-80	H	SHORT	7-15-80	27.4597	7-18-80	28.6888	2005-	2	1522	1	1441-	4 S
9-80	H END	LONG	7-18-80	28.6888	7-31-80	30.0500	1163-	1	2868	2	1459	11 L
3-81	H	LONG	7-31-80	32.2500	8-15-80	34.8937	0	1	5656	9	2895	11 L
3-81	H	SHORT	8-15-80	34.8937	8-29-80	35.0438	1911-	3	2568	10	233-	7 S
3-81	H MO	LONG	8-29-80	35.0438	9-29-80	39.7296	1281-	3	8014	7	5183	21 L
3-81	H	SHORT	9-29-80	39.7296	10- 1-80	42.6600	3282-	2	1052	20	3347	3 S
3-81	H	LONG	10- 1-80	42.6600	10-15-80	43.3574	1131-	3	3180	3	716	11 L
3-81	H	SHORT	10-15-80	43.3574	10-17-80	45.2700	2142-	3	736	10	2207-	3 S
3-81	H MO	LONG	10-17-80	45.2700	10-21-80	43.4083	2085-	3	89	1	2150-	3 L
3-81	H	SHORT	10-21-80	43.4083	10-30-80	43.5292	1755-	2	2865	1	200-	3 S
3-81	H	LONG	10-30-80	43.5292	11- 7-80	42.8200	1768-	1	2487	6	859-	6 L
3-81	H	SHORT	11- 7-80	42.8200	12-15-80	29.1517	1265-	1	20518	4	15243	26 S
3-81	H MO	LONG	12-15-80	29.1517	12-29-80	30.7226	729-	1	4254	25	1694	9 L
3-81	H	SHORT	12-29-80	30.7226	1- 5-81	31.9000	1318-	4	2433	7	1383-	4 S
3-81	H	LONG	1- 5-81	31.9000	1-12-81	30.8700	1153-	6	2184	2	1218-	6 L
3-81	H	SHORT	1-12-81	30.8700	1-23-81	28.7162	425-	1	5286	6	2347	10 S
3-81	H	LONG	1-23-81	28.7162	1-29-81	27.4381	1431-	5	1381	1	1496-	5 L
3-81	H END	SHORT	1-29-81	27.4381	1-30-81	26.7900	181-	1	1386	5	660	3 S
9-81	H ENDMO	SHORT	1-30-81	26.9600	2- 9-81	28.1600	1344-	6	2430	3	1409-	6 S
9-81	H MO	LONG	2- 9-81	28.1600	2-18-81	24.3600	4323-	7	0	4	4388-	7 L
9-81	H	SHORT	2-18-81	24.3000	5-21-81	16.1448	1064-	3	11032	59	9068	66 S
9-81	H	LONG	5-21-81	16.1448	6- 4-81	16.9356	1058-	1	3645	7	820	10 L
9-81	H	SHORT	6- 4-81	16.9356	7-10-81	16.6596	1248-	3	2055	20	244	26 S

76

WORLD SUGAR

DELIV	RULE	POSITION	DATE-IN	PRICE-IN	DATE-OUT	PRICE-OUT	MAX-LOSS	DAYS	MAX-GAIN	DAYS	NET-PROFIT	DAYS	L/S
9-81	M	LONG	7-10-81	16.6596	7-20-81	15.6792	1098-	7	1165	3	1163-	7	L
9-81	M END	SHORT	7-20-81	15.6792	7-31-81	16.7000	1804-	6	32	1	1208-	11	S
3-82	ENDM	SHORT	7-31-81	16.9800	9-24-81	13.5719	0	1	5857	27	3752	38	S
3-82	M	LONG	9-24-81	13.5719	10-19-81	12.0295	1727-	18	31	1	1792-	18	L
3-82	M	SHORT	10-19-81	12.0295	11-25-81	12.7107	862-	12	593	6	827-	28	S
3-82	M	LONG	11-25-81	12.7107	1-4-82	12.7593	370-	1	1511	19	10-	25	L
3-82	M MO	SHORT	1-4-82	12.7593	1-27-82	14.0000	1389-	18	133	1	1454-	18	S
3-82	MO END	LONG	1-27-82	14.0000	1-29-82	13.5800	582-	3	112	2	535-	4	L
9-82	ENDM	LONG	1-29-82	14.0800	2-22-82	13.4858	665-	15	246	2	730-	15	L
9-82	M	SHORT	2-22-82	13.4858	6-30-82	7.8804	127-	1	7376	81	6213	91	S
9-82	M	LONG	6-30-82	7.8804	7-20-82	7.7843	291-	1	1993	10	172-	14	L
9-82	M END	SHORT	7-20-82	7.7843	7-30-82	7.4900	510-	1	788	8	264	10	S
3-83	ENDM	SHORT	7-30-82	8.7800	10-29-82	7.7086	212-	2	2441	46	1134	64	S
3-83	M MO	LONG	10-29-82	7.7086	12-9-82	7.0800	704-	28	695	21	769-	28	L
3-83	MO END	SHORT	12-9-82	7.0800	1-31-83	6.2000	257-	1	1153	24	920	9	S
9-83	ENDM	SHORT	1-31-83	7.3400	2-11-83	7.9457	678-	9	44	1	743-	7	S
9-83	M MO	LONG	2-11-83	7.9457	2-28-83	6.8700	1204-	11	273	2	1269-	11	L
9-83	M	SHORT	2-28-83	6.8700	4-4-83	7.8779	1128-	25	78	2	1193-	25	S
9-83	M	LONG	4-4-83	7.8779	6-2-83	11.0634	400-	8	6610	41	3502	43	L
9-83	M	SHORT	6-2-83	11.0634	6-23-83	11.6869	1552-	2	1123	12	763-	16	S
9-83	M	LONG	6-23-83	11.6869	7-15-83	10.2140	1649-	16	205	4	1714-	16	L
9-83	M	SHORT	7-15-83	10.2140	7-22-83	11.1054	998-	6	799	2	1063-	6	S
9-83	M END	LONG	7-22-83	11.1054	7-29-83	11.2900	678-	1	867	3	141	7	L
3-84	ENDM	LONG	7-29-83	12.7900	9-14-83	11.0482	1950-	32	728	2	2015-	32	L
3-84	M	SHORT	9-14-83	11.0482	10-6-83	11.7647	802-	17	636	9	867-	17	S
3-84	M	LONG	10-6-83	11.7647	10-20-83	10.5988	1305-	11	196	3	1370-	11	L
3-84	M END	SHORT	10-20-83	10.5988	1-31-84	7.5000	202-	3	3739	66	3405	72	S
9-84	ENDEND	SHORT	1-31-84	8.4000	7-31-84	4.4000	89-	3	4536	117	4415	127	S
3-85	ENDMO	SHORT	7-31-84	5.7200	8-28-84	5.9800	291-	20	873	11	356-	20	S
3-85	MO M	LONG	8-28-84	5.9800	9-17-84	5.1230	959-	14	212	6	1024-	14	L
3-85	M MO	SHORT	9-17-84	5.1230	10-3-84	5.9900	971-	13	81	1	1036-	13	S
3-85	MO M	LONG	10-3-84	5.9900	11-19-84	5.2894	784-	34	313	6	849-	34	L
3-85	M	SHORT	11-19-84	5.2894	1-14-85	4.8378	168-	8	1432	31	440	37	S
3-85	M END	LONG	1-14-85	4.8378	1-31-85	4.3200	915-	5	2	1	644-	15	L

TOTALS FOR ALL CONTRACTS OF: WORLD SUGAR

NET PROFIT = 28731	NUM TRADES = 89	LARGEST PROFIT = 15243	AV PROFIT TRADE= 3222
TOTAL PROFITS = 103107	NUM WINS = 32	LARGEST LOSS = 4388-	AV LOSS TRADE= 1304-
TOTAL LOSSES = 74376-	NUM LOSSES = 57	BEST POSITION = 20518	AV DAYS IN WIN = 38
PROFIT FACTOR = 1.38	PERCENT WINS = 36	WORST POSITION = 4323-	AV DAYS IN LOSS= 11
MAX DRAWDOWN = 8047-	MARGIN = 1200	AV BEST POSITION= 2410	NUM MONTHS = 83
AV NET PROFIT = 322	RETURN ON CAP= 31	AV WORST POSITION= 1088-	PROFIT/DRAWDOWN= 3.57

REL PROFIT FACTOR=	-.86
AV PROFIT/AV LOSS=	2.47
MAX WINS IN ROW=	3
MAX LOSSES IN ROW=	6
DAY COMMISSION =	65
NIGHT COMMISSION =	65

77

IMM T-BILLS

DELIV	RULE	POSITION	DATE-IN	PRICE-IN	DATE-OUT	PRICE-OUT	MAX-LOSS	DAYS	MAX-GAIN	DAYS	NET-PROFIT	DAYS	
12-78	M END	SHORT	10-30-78	91.1900	11-30-78	90.9300	725-	1	1425	4	585	22	S
6-79	ENDEND	SHORT	11-30-78	90.6200	5-31-79	90.6000	650-	44	1200	14	15-	126	S
12-79	ENDM	SHORT	5-31-79	91.2800	6- 6-79	91.5700	725-	4	375	2	790-	4	S
12-79	M M	LONG	6- 6-79	91.5700	9- 5-79	89.9600	4025-	64	1725	16	4090-	64	L
12-79	M M	SHORT	9- 5-79	89.9600	11-12-79	88.7300	1350-	13	7450	34	3010	49	S
12-79	M END	LONG	11-12-79	88.7300	11-30-79	88.8000	1925-	3	2475	11	110	15	L
6-80	ENDM	LONG	11-30-79	90.5500	12-12-79	89.4500	2750-	8	1150	5	2815-	8	L
6-80	M M	SHORT	12-12-79	89.4500	4- 3-80	86.3700	2625-	19	13125	71	7635	78	S
6-80	M END	LONG	4- 3-80	86.3700	5-30-80	92.3000	1775-	1	15900	37	14760	41	L
12-80	ENDM	LONG	5-30-80	92.3000	7-31-80	91.0300	2225-	43	3425	10	2290-	43	L
12-80	M END	SHORT	7-31-80	91.0300	11-28-80	85.8700	875-	6	13025	81	12835	85	S
6-81	ENDM	SHORT	11-28-80	85.8700	12-19-80	87.4700	1050-	4	4625	10	615-	15	S
6-81	M M	LONG	12-19-80	87.4700	2- 9-81	87.6100	400-	15	4900	10	285	34	L
6-81	M M	SHORT	2- 9-81	87.6100	3-12-81	88.4600	2125-	23	3125	5	2190-	23	S
6-81	M M	LONG	3-12-81	88.4600	4- 6-81	87.2300	3075-	18	2300	5	3140-	18	L
6-81	M END	SHORT	4- 6-81	87.2300	5-28-81	85.0400	1475-	3	9700	28	5410	37	S
12-81	ENDM	LONG	5-28-81	85.0400	5-29-81	85.3900	1225-	1	900	2	810	3	L
12-81	M M	SHORT	5-29-81	85.3900	7- 7-81	86.7100	2225-	26	1700	11	2390-	26	S
12-81	M M	LONG	7- 7-81	86.7100	9-11-81	86.1100	2650-	4	4975	46	1435	48	L
6-82	ENDM	LONG	9-11-81	86.1100	11-30-81	89.5300	2975-	15	9575	54	8485	57	L
6-82	M M	SHORT	11-30-81	89.1900	12-10-81	88.1200	2675-	8	650	5	2740-	8	S
6-82	M M	LONG	12-10-81	88.1200	2-22-82	86.9000	1250-	1	6675	46	2985	50	L
6-82	M M	SHORT	2-22-82	86.9000	3-29-82	86.5800	800-	26	3550	11	865-	26	S
6-82	M END	LONG	3-29-82	86.5800	5- 7-82	88.3700	4475-	29	300	2	4540-	29	L
12-82	ENDM	LONG	5- 7-82	88.3700	5-28-82	88.5700	1375-	8	1425	11	435	17	L
12-82	M M	SHORT	5-28-82	88.0200	6-14-82	86.8500	2925-	10	0	1	2990-	10	S
12-82	M END	LONG	6-14-82	86.8500	7- 8-82	87.5800	1825-	18	1450	10	1890-	18	L
12-82	M END	LONG	7- 8-82	87.5800	11-30-82	91.7500	925-	1	12650	73	10360	103	L
6-83	ENDEND	LONG	11-30-82	90.6100	5-31-83	91.3000	0	1	4475	61	1660	127	L
12-83	ENDEND	LONG	5-31-83	90.7300	11-30-83	91.0700	2650-	48	1525	98	785	128	L
6-84	ENDEND	LONG	11-30-83	90.3900	5-31-84	90.1800	2375-	113	1075	30	590-	127	L
12-84	ENDEND	LONG	5-31-84	87.8400	11-30-84	91.5400	0	1	9825	123	9185	129	L
6-85	ENDM	LONG	11-30-84	90.7000	3- 1-85	90.6700	75-	62	2775	38	140-	62	L
6-85	M M	SHORT	3- 1-85	90.6700	4-16-85	92.0600	3475-	32	700	5	3540-	32	S
6-85	M END	LONG	4-16-85	92.0600	4-26-85	92.0300	600-	1	475	3	140-	10	L

TOTALS FOR ALL CONTRACTS OF: IMM T-BILLS

NET PROFIT = 45000	NUM TRADES = 35	LARGEST PROFIT = 14760	AV PROFIT TRADE = 4751	REL PROFIT FACTOR= 1.14
TOTAL PROFITS = 80770	NUM WINS = 17	LARGEST LOSS = 4540-	AV LOSS TRADE= 1987-	AV PROFIT/AV LOSS= 2.39
TOTAL LOSSES = 35770-	NUM LOSSES = 18	BEST POSITION = 15900	AV DAYS IN WIN = 60	MAX WINS IN ROW = 3
PROFIT FACTOR = 2.25	PERCENT WINS = 49	WORST POSITION = 4475-	AV DAYS IN LOSS = 36	MAX LOSSES IN ROW = 3
MAX DRAWDOWN = 9850-	MARGIN = 1500	AV BEST POSITION = 4392	NUM MONTHS = 78	DAY COMMISSION = 65
AV NET PROFIT = 1285	RETURN ON CAP= 44	AV WORST POSITION= 1692-	PROFIT/DRAWDOWN= 4.56	NIGHT COMMISSION = 65

All Futures Contracts Combined Chronologically— Trade-By-Trade

COMMODITY	DELIV	POSITION	DATE-IN	PRICE-IN	DATE-OUT	PRICE-OUT	NET-PROFIT	CUM-PROFIT
1 PORK BELLIES	2-78	LONG	1- 4-78	59.6405	1-31-78	63.6500	1378	1378
1 COMEX SILVER	3-77	SHORT	12-30-77	485.0000	2-28-78	496.0000	615-	763
5 SOYBEANS	7-78	SHORT	1-17-78	575.5000	3- 1-78	616.5000	2115-	1352-
1 SOYBEAN MEAL	7-78	SHORT	1-17-78	157.8000	3- 8-78	173.1000	1595-	2947-
1 PORK BELLIES	7-78	LONG	1-31-78	61.5500	3-20-78	76.4849	5311	2364
1 COFFEE	7-78	SHORT	1-24-78	163.1000	3-28-78	147.8600	5650	8014
1 PORK BELLIES	7-78	SHORT	3-20-78	76.4849	3-28-78	84.0000	2770-	5244
1 PORK BELLIES	7-78	LONG	3-28-78	84.0000	4-10-78	77.4182	2434-	2810
1 JAPANESE YEN	6-78	LONG	3-16-78	.4388	4-21-78	.4448	685	3495
1 JAPANESE YEN	6-78	SHORT	4-21-78	.4448	5-31-78	.4560	1465-	2030
1 JAPANESE YEN	6-78	LONG	5-31-78	.4560		.4560	65-	1965
1 COFFEE	7-78	LONG	3-28-78	147.8600	6-12-78	165.5000	6550	8515
5 SOYBEANS	7-78	LONG	3- 1-78	616.5030	6-14-78	665.0000	2360	10875
1 PLATINUM	7-78	LONG	1-23-78	218.1000	6-30-78	238.2000	940	11815
1 SOYBEAN MEAL	7-78	LONG	3- 8-78	173.1000	6-30-78	174.8000	105	11920
1 PORK BELLIES	7-78	SHORT	4-10-78	77.4182	6-30-78	50.0500	9787	21707
1 COFFEE	7-78	SHORT	6-12-78	165.5000	6-30-78	158.3800	2605	24312
5 SOYBEANS	7-78	SHORT	6-14-78	665.0000	6-30-78	685.0000	1065-	23247
1 PORK BELLIES	2-79	SHORT	6-14-78	54.4000	7-27-78	58.8000	1737-	21510
1 WORLD SUGAR	9-78	SHORT	2- 8-78	9.6124	7-31-78	6.3500	3588	25098
1 COFFEE	12-78	SHORT	7- 3-78	132.5000	7-31-78	121.1700	4183	29281
1 WORLD SUGAR	3-79	SHORT	7-31-78	6.9000	8- 7-78	7.7238	987-	28294
5 SOYBEANS	11-78	SHORT	6-30-78	630.5000	8-15-78	636.0000	340-	27954
1 COMEX SILVER	9-78	SHORT	2-28-78	517.5000	8-31-78	548.0000	1590-	26364
1 COPPER	9-78	LONG	5-25-78	66.0332	8-31-78	63.4000	723-	25641
1 JAPANESE YEN	9-78	LONG	5-31-78	.4624	8-31-78	.5225	7447	33088
1 PORK BELLIES	2-79	LONG	7-27-78	58.8000	9-13-78	57.1608	687-	32401
1 PORK BELLIES	2-79	SHORT	9-13-78	57.1608	9-19-78	62.9500	2264-	30137
1 WORLD SUGAR	3-79	LONG	8- 7-78	7.7238	10-17-78	8.7509	1085	31222
1 PORK BELLIES	2-79	LONG	9-19-78	62.9500	10-20-78	67.6843	1734	32956
1 WORLD SUGAR	3-79	SHORT	10-17-78	8.7509	10-26-78	9.7043	1132-	31824
1 COMEX SILVER	11-78	LONG	8-31-78	572.0000	10-30-78	650.0000	3965-	27859
5 SOYBEANS	11-78	LONG	8-15-78	636.0000	10-31-78	707.2500	3497	31356
1 JAPANESE YEN	12-78	SHORT	8-31-78	.5311	11- 2-78	.5379	785	32141
1 WORLD SUGAR	3-79	LONG	10-26-78	9.7043	11- 8-78	8.7332	1152-	30989
1 PLATINUM	1-79	LONG	6-30-78	244.5000	11-10-78	316.6000	3540	34529
1 COFFEE	12-78	LONG	7-31-78	121.1000	11-15-78	144.0000	8496	43025
1 PORK BELLIES	2-79	SHORT	10-20-78	67.6843	11-22-78	67.9313	158-	42867
1 SOYBEAN MEAL	12-78	LONG	6-30-78	171.1000	11-30-78	185.1000	1335	44202
1 IMM T-BILLS	12-78	SHORT	10-30-78	91.1900	11-30-78	90.9300	585	44787
1 JAPANESE YEN	12-78	SHORT	11- 2-78	.5379	11-30-78	.5048	4072	48859
1 COFFEE	12-78	LONG	11-15-78	144.0000	12-11-78	141.7500	778	49637
1 PORK BELLIES	2-79	SHORT	11-22-78	67.9313	12-11-78	63.6768	1681-	47956
1 COFFEE	7-79	LONG	11-30-78	128.2500	12-26-78	129.2500	440-	47516
1 PLATINUM	1-79	SHORT	11-10-78	316.6000	12-29-78	349.0000	1685-	45831

TOTALS FOR THE YEAR 1978:

NET PROFIT FOR YEAR=	45831
EQUITY ON JANUARY 1=	100000
EQUITY ON DECEMBER 31=	145831
PER CENT GAIN ON ORIGINAL EQUITY=	46
TOTAL NUMBER OF TRADES FOR YEAR=	45
NUMBER OF PROFITABLE TRADES FOR YEAR=	23
NUMBER OF LOSING TRADES FOR YEAR=	22
PER CENT PROFITABLE TRADES FOR YEAR=	51
MAXIMUM DRAWDOWN FOR YEAR=	6049-
PROFIT FACTOR FOR YEAR=	2.49
RELATIVE PROFIT FACTOR FOR YEAR=	1.21

COMMODITY	DELIV	POSITION	DATE-IN	PRICE-IN	DATE-OUT	PRICE-OUT	NET-PROFIT	CUM-PROFIT
1 COFFEE	7-79	LONG	12-26-78	129.2500	1-11-79	124.1600	1973-	43858
1 PORK BELLIES	2-79	SHORT	12-11-78	63.6768	1-24-79	61.2123	871	44729
1 PLATINUM	7-79	SHORT	12-29-78	357.6000	1-24-79	387.4000	1555-	43174
1 WORLD SUGAR	3-79	SHORT	11-8-78	8.7332	1-24-79	8.2200	509	43683
1 PORK BELLIES	2-79	LONG	1-24-79	61.2123	1-31-79	63.7000	880	44563
1 COPPER	3-79	LONG	8-31-78	66.7500	1-31-79	91.3500	6085	50648
1 COMEX SILVER	3-79	LONG	10-30-78	650.0000	2-28-79	771.0000	5985	56633
1 JAPANESE YEN	3-79	SHORT	11-30-78	.5167	2-28-79	.4969	2410	59043
1 COFFEE	7-79	SHORT	1-11-79	124.1600	3-5-79	132.2000	3080-	55963
1 PLATINUM	7-79	LONG	1-24-79	387.4000	3-6-79	384.0000	235-	55728
1 PORK BELLIES	7-79	LONG	1-31-79	63.5000	3-6-79	64.1245	172	55900
1 PORK BELLIES	7-79	SHORT	3-6-79	64.1245	4-27-79	60.8877	1164	57064
1 PLATINUM	7-79	SHORT	3-6-79	384.0000	4-30-79	408.5000	1290-	55774
1 PORK BELLIES	7-79	LONG	4-27-79	60.8877	5-4-79	56.5655	1707-	54067
1 COPPER	9-79	LONG	2-28-79	93.1500	5-8-79	85.6492	1940-	52127
1 JAPANESE YEN	6-79	SHORT	5-9-79	.5046	5-29-79	.4728	3910	56037
1 JAPANESE YEN	6-79	LONG	5-29-79	.4728	5-31-79	.4513	2752-	53285
1 IMM T-BILLS	6-79	LONG	11-30-78	90.6200	5-31-79	90.6000	390-	52880
1 WORLD SUGAR	6-79	SHORT	1-31-79	9.0000	6-4-79	8.8851	63	52943
1 IMM T-BILLS	12-79	SHORT	5-31-79	91.2800	6-6-79	91.5700	790-	52153
1 JAPANESE YEN	9-79	SHORT	5-31-79	.4590	6-25-79	.4752	2090-	50063
5 SOYBEANS	7-79	LONG	10-31-78	736.5000	6-29-79	741.5000	185	50248
1 SOYBEAN MEAL	7-79	LONG	11-30-78	187.1000	6-29-79	199.2000	1145	51393
1 COFFEE	7-79	LONG	3-5-79	132.2000	6-29-79	215.2300	31071	82464
1 PLATINUM	7-79	LONG	4-30-79	408.5000	6-29-79	423.0000	660	83124
1 PORK BELLIES	7-79	SHORT	5-4-79	56.5655	6-29-79	35.2750	8025	91149
5 SOYBEANS	7-79	SHORT	6-29-79	741.5000	6-29-79	741.5000	65-	91084
1 SOYBEAN MEAL	7-79	SHORT	6-29-79	199.2000	6-29-79	199.2000	65-	91019
1 COFFEE	12-79	LONG	6-29-79	220.0000	7-13-79	203.2200	6357-	84662
1 WORLD SUGAR	9-79	LONG	6-4-79	8.8851	7-23-79	8.4379	565-	84097
1 PLATINUM	1-80	LONG	6-29-79	423.9000	7-30-79	388.3000	1845-	82252
1 WORLD SUGAR	9-79	SHORT	7-23-79	8.4379	7-31-79	8.4700	100-	82152
1 PORK BELLIES	2-80	SHORT	6-29-79	42.5750	8-13-79	42.2696	51	82203
1 COPPER	9-79	SHORT	5-8-79	85.6492	8-15-79	90.4552	1266-	80937
1 COFFEE	12-79	SHORT	7-13-79	203.2200	8-15-79	195.3400	2890	83827
1 PLATINUM	1-80	SHORT	7-30-79	388.3000	8-23-79	417.8000	1540-	82287
1 JAPANESE YEN	9-79	LONG	6-29-79	.4752	8-31-79	.4506	3140-	79147
1 COMEX SILVER	9-79	LONG	2-28-79	801.0000	8-31-79	1061.5000	12960	92107
1 IMM T-BILLS	9-79	LONG	8-15-79	90.4552	8-31-79	90.0000	178-	91929
1 JAPANESE YEN	9-79	SHORT	8-29-79	.4506	8-31-79	.4570	865-	91064
1 IMM T-BILLS	12-79	LONG	6-6-79	91.5700	9-5-79	89.9600	4090-	86974
1 WORLD SUGAR	3-80	SHORT	7-31-79	10.0700	9-5-79	11.0009	1107-	85867
1 PORK BELLIES	2-80	LONG	8-13-79	42.2696	9-25-79	43.6078	443	86310
1 COFFEE	12-79	LONG	8-15-79	195.3400	10-12-79	208.1800	4750	91060
1 PLATINUM	1-80	LONG	8-23-79	417.8000	10-15-79	500.2000	4055	95115
1 COPPER	12-79	LONG	8-15-79	92.9500	10-16-79	89.0389	1042-	94073
1 COFFEE	1-80	SHORT	10-12-79	208.1800	10-19-79	216.9800	3365-	90708
1 PORK BELLIES	3-80	SHORT	9-25-79	43.6078	10-23-79	46.1143	1017-	89691
5 SOYBEANS	12-79	SHORT	6-29-79	739.0000	10-31-79	645.0000	4635	94326
1 PLATINUM	2-80	SHORT	10-15-79	500.2000	11-12-79	523.6000	1235-	93091
1 IMM T-BILLS	1-80	SHORT	9-5-79	89.9600	11-15-79	88.7300	3010	96101
1 SOYBEAN MEAL	12-79	SHORT	6-29-79	198.5000	11-15-79	195.9000	195	96296

COMMODITY	DELIV	POSITION	DATE-IN	PRICE-IN	DATE-OUT	PRICE-OUT	NET-PROFIT	CUM-PROFIT
1 COPPER	3-80	SHORT	10-16-79	89.0389	11-19-79	101.1063	3081-	93215
1 PORK BELLIES	2-80	LONG	10-23-79	46.1143	11-29-79	49.5982	1258	94473
1 JAPANESE YEN	12-79	SHORT	8-31-79	.4626	11-30-79	.4017	7547	102020
1 COFFEE	12-79	LONG	10-19-79	216.9800	11-30-79	220.0900	1101	103121
1 IMM T-BILLS	12-79	LONG	11-12-79	88.7300	11-30-79	88.8000	110	103231
1 SOYBEAN MEAL	12-79	LONG	11-15-79	195.9000	11-30-79	196.8000	25	103256
1 COFFEE	7-80	LONG	11-30-79	189.6000	11-30-79	185.6000	1565-	101691
1 JAPANESE YEN	3-80	SHORT	11-30-79	.4068	12- 7-79	.4236	2165-	99526
1 WORLD SUGAR	3-80	LONG	9- 5-79	11.0009	12-10-79	15.5036	4978	104504
1 IMM T-BILLS	6-80	LONG	11-30-79	90.5500	12-12-79	89.4500	2815-	101689
1 WORLD SUGAR	3-80	SHORT	12-10-79	15.5036	12-18-79	16.8065	1524-	100165
1 PLATINUM	1-80	LONG	11- 7-79	523.6000	12-28-79	692.6000	8385	108550

TOTALS FOR THE YEAR 1979:

NET PROFIT FOR YEAR=	62719
EQUITY ON JANUARY 1=	145831
EQUITY ON DECEMBER 31=	208550
PER CENT GAIN ON ORIGINAL EQUITY=	63
TOTAL NUMBER OF TRADES FOR YEAR=	65
NUMBER OF PROFITABLE TRADES FOR YEAR=	31
NUMBER OF LOSING TRADES FOR YEAR=	34
PER CENT PROFITABLE TRADES FOR YEAR=	48
MAXIMUM DRAWDOWN FOR YEAR=	12002-
PROFIT FACTOR FOR YEAR=	2.10
RELATIVE PROFIT FACTOR FOR YEAR=	1.08

COMMODITY	DELIV	POSITION	DATE-IN	PRICE-IN	DATE-OUT	PRICE-OUT	NET-PROFIT	CUM-PROFIT
1 WORLD SUGAR	3-80	LONG	12-18-79	16.8065	1- 2-80	15.6832	1323-	107227
1 SOYBEAN MEAL	7-80	LONG	11-30-79	202.0000	1- 9-80	186.3000	1635-	105592
1 WORLD SUGAR	3-80	SHORT	1- 2-80	15.6832	1-11-80	16.6601	1159-	104433
1 COMEX SILVER	3-80	LONG	8-31-79	1104.5000	1-24-80	3850.0000	137210	241643
1 COMEX GOLD	2-80	LONG	9-10-79	355.3000	1-24-80	684.0000	32805	274448
1 PLATINUM	7-80	LONG	1- 3-80	767.5000	1-24-80	835.2000	3320	277768
1 WORLD SUGAR	3-80	LONG	1-11-80	16.6601	1-28-80	18.6880	2206	279974
1 WORLD SUGAR	3-80	SHORT	1-28-80	18.6880	1-29-80	20.2365	1799-	278175
1 PORK BELLIES	2-80	SHORT	11-29-79	49.5982	1-31-80	40.5000	3392	281567
1 COMEX GOLD	2-80	SHORT	1-24-80	684.0000	1-31-80	681.5000	185	281752
1 WORLD SUGAR	3-80	LONG	1-29-80	20.2365	1-31-80	22.0100	1921	283673
1 PLATINUM	7-80	SHORT	1-24-80	835.2000	2- 4-80	896.0000	3105-	280568
1 COMEX SILVER	3-80	SHORT	1-24-80	3850.0000	2-13-80	3675.0000	8685	289253
1 HEATING OIL #2	8-80	LONG	1-30-80	90.5000	2-13-80	82.6000	3383-	285870
1 COMEX SILVER	3-80	LONG	2- 7-80	3675.0000	2-14-80	3660.0000	815-	285055
1 COFFEE	7-80	SHORT	11-30-79	185.6000	2-19-80	179.6400	2170	287225
1 JAPANESE YEN	3-80	LONG	11-19-79	.4236	2-19-80	.4086	1940-	285285
1 COPPER	3-80	LONG	1-31-80	101.1063	2-20-80	123.7000	5583	290868
1 WORLD SUGAR	9-80	LONG	2-26-80	22.2400	2-26-80	24.9996	3025	293893
1 WORLD SUGAR	9-80	SHORT	2-26-80	24.9996	2-27-80	26.9000	2193-	291700
1 COMEX SILVER	3-80	SHORT	2-14-80	3660.0000	2-28-80	3520.0000	6935	298635
1 WORLD SUGAR	9-80	LONG	2-27-80	26.9000	2-28-80	24.8032	2413-	296222
1 JAPANESE YEN	3-80	SHORT	2-19-80	.4086	2-29-80	.3980	1260	297482
1 COPPER	3-80	SHORT	2-20-80	123.7000	2-29-80	119.5000	985	298467
1 COMEX SILVER	3-80	LONG	2-28-80	3520.0000	2-29-80	3530.0000	435	298902
1 WORLD SUGAR	9-80	SHORT	2-28-80	24.8032	2-29-80	26.9000	2413-	296489
1 PORK BELLIES	7-80	SHORT	1-31-80	45.2750	3- 3-80	45.4886	146-	296343
1 COMEX SILVER	9-80	LONG	2-29-80	3784.0000	3- 7-80	3647.0000	6915-	289428
1 WORLD SUGAR	9-80	LONG	2-29-80	26.9000	3- 7-80	26.6000	401-	289027
1 PLATINUM	7-80	LONG	2- 4-80	896.0000	3-10-80	951.5000	2710	291737
1 WORLD SUGAR	9-80	SHORT	3- 7-80	26.6000	3-24-80	23.2891	3643	295380
1 PORK BELLIES	7-80	LONG	3- 3-80	45.4886	3-25-80	40.8000	1846-	293534
1 WORLD SUGAR	9-80	LONG	3-24-80	23.2891	3-25-80	21.3807	2202-	291332
1 COFFEE	7-80	LONG	2-19-80	179.6400	3-28-80	189.1600	3505	294837
1 IMM T-BILLS	6-80	SHORT	12-19-79	89.4500	4- 3-80	86.3700	7635	302472
1 HEATING OIL #2	8-80	SHORT	2-13-80	82.6000	4- 3-80	82.0000	187	302659
1 WORLD SUGAR	9-80	SHORT	3-25-80	21.3807	4- 3-80	22.0953	865-	301794
1 JAPANESE YEN	6-80	SHORT	2-29-80	.4035	4-23-80	.4133	1290-	300504
1 PLATINUM	7-80	LONG	3-10-80	951.5000	4-25-80	622.0000	16410	316914
1 PLATINUM	7-80	SHORT	4-25-80	622.0000	5- 1-80	546.2000	3855-	313059
1 COFFEE	7-80	SHORT	3-28-80	189.1600	5- 5-80	194.9400	2232-	310827
1 WORLD SUGAR	9-80	LONG	4- 3-80	22.0953	5-21-80	32.7540	11872	322699
1 COPPER	9-80	SHORT	2-29-80	128.0000	5-23-80	96.5593	7795	330494
1 WORLD SUGAR	9-80	SHORT	5-21-80	32.7540	5-27-80	35.9900	3689-	326805
1 COMEX GOLD	8-80	SHORT	1-31-80	748.0000	5-30-80	555.0000	19235	346040
1 COMEX SILVER	9-80	SHORT	3- 7-80	3647.0000	5-30-80	1417.0000	111435	457475
1 IMM T-BILLS	6-80	LONG	4- 3-80	86.3700	5-30-80	92.3000	14760	472235
1 JAPANESE YEN	6-80	LONG	4-23-80	.4133	5-30-80	.4474	4197	476432
1 PLATINUM	7-80	SHORT	5- 1-80	546.2000	5-27-80	595.3000	2520-	473912
1 WORLD SUGAR	9-80	LONG	5-27-80	35.9900	6- 3-80	33.9100	2394-	471518
1 COPPER	9-80	LONG	5-23-80	96.5593	6-10-80	87.0528	2441-	469077
1 WORLD SUGAR	9-80	LONG	6- 3-80	33.9100	6-12-80	34.5400	770-	468307
1 HEATING OIL #2	8-80	LONG	4- 3-80	82.0000	6-16-80	78.1000	1703-	466604

QTY	COMMODITY	DELIV	POSITION	DATE-IN	PRICE-IN	DATE-OUT	PRICE-OUT	NET-PROFIT	CUM-PROFIT
1	COFFEE	9-80	LONG	5-5-80	194.9400	6-16-80	182.6100	4688-	461916
1	WORLD SUGAR	9-80	LONG	6-12-80	34.5400	6-24-80	34.4469	169-	461747
1	PORK BELLIES	7-80	SHORT	3-25-80	40.8000	6-25-80	34.9500	2158	463905
5	SOYBEANS	7-80	SHORT	10-31-79	725.2500	6-30-80	671.0000	2647	466552
1	SOYBEAN MEAL	7-80	SHORT	1-9-80	186.3000	6-30-80	179.4000	625	467177
1	PLATINUM	7-80	LONG	5-30-80	595.3000	6-30-80	676.2000	3980	471157
1	COPPER	9-80	SHORT	6-10-80	87.0528	6-30-80	93.9482	1788-	469369
1	COFFEE	9-80	SHORT	6-16-80	182.6100	6-30-80	168.0500	5395	474764
1	HEATING OIL #2	8-80	SHORT	6-16-80	78.1000	6-30-80	76.8400	464	475228
1	PORK BELLIES	7-80	LONG	6-25-80	34.9500	6-30-80	38.8000	1398	476626
5	SOYBEANS	7-80	LONG	6-30-80	671.0000	6-30-80	671.0000	65-	476561
1	SOYBEAN MEAL	12-80	SHORT	6-30-80	193.7000	7-2-80	203.2000	1015-	475546
1	WORLD SUGAR	9-80	SHORT	6-24-80	34.4469	7-14-80	29.2971	5702	481248
1	COMEX SILVER	8-80	LONG	5-30-80	1417.0000	7-15-80	1555.0000	6835	488083
1	COMEX GOLD	8-80	LONG	5-30-80	555.0000	7-15-80	620.5000	6485	494568
1	PLATINUM	1-81	LONG	6-30-80	719.2000	7-15-80	675.0000	2275-	492293
1	WORLD SUGAR	9-80	LONG	7-14-80	29.2971	7-15-80	27.4597	2122-	490171
1	WORLD SUGAR	9-80	SHORT	7-15-80	27.4597	7-18-80	28.6888	1441-	488730
1	JAPANESE YEN	9-80	LONG	5-30-80	.4461	7-23-80	.4430	452-	488278
1	COPPER	9-80	LONG	6-30-80	93.9482	7-30-80	94.8086	150	488428
1	IMM T-BILLS	12-80	LONG	5-30-80	91.9200	7-31-80	91.0300	2290-	486138
1	COMEX GOLD	8-80	SHORT	7-15-80	620.5000	7-31-80	619.7000	15	486153
1	WORLD SUGAR	9-80	SHORT	7-18-80	28.6888	7-31-80	30.0500	1459	487612
1	COFFEE	12-80	SHORT	6-30-80	181.8100	8-6-80	156.0200	9606	497218
1	WORLD SUGAR	3-81	LONG	7-31-80	32.2500	8-15-80	34.8937	2895	500113
1	PLATINUM	1-81	SHORT	7-15-80	675.0000	8-20-80	691.6000	895-	499218
1	PORK BELLIES	2-81	LONG	6-30-80	53.0250	8-25-80	58.3922	1974	501192
1	COFFEE	12-80	LONG	8-6-80	156.0200	8-25-80	136.2500	7478-	493714
1	JAPANESE YEN	9-80	SHORT	7-23-80	.4430	8-26-80	.4563	1727-	491987
1	COMEX SILVER	9-80	SHORT	7-15-80	1555.0000	8-29-80	1630.0000	3815-	488172
1	COPPER	9-80	SHORT	7-30-80	94.8086	8-29-80	87.2000	1837	490009
1	WORLD SUGAR	3-81	SHORT	8-15-80	34.8937	8-29-80	35.0438	233-	489776
1	JAPANESE YEN	9-80	LONG	8-26-80	.4563	8-29-80	.4575	85	489861
1	PORK BELLIES	2-81	SHORT	8-25-80	58.3922	9-4-80	63.1367	1867-	487994
1	COMEX SILVER	3-81	SHORT	8-29-80	1744.0000	9-4-80	1787.5000	2240-	485754
1	COMEX GOLD	2-81	SHORT	7-31-80	654.7000	9-8-80	711.2000	5715-	480039
1	COFFEE	12-80	SHORT	8-25-80	136.2500	9-9-80	143.3400	2723-	477316
1	COPPER	3-81	SHORT	8-29-80	92.6500	9-11-80	100.5421	2038-	475278
1	COFFEE	12-80	LONG	9-9-80	143.3400	9-15-80	130.2600	4970-	470308
1	HEATING OIL #2	2-81	SHORT	8-29-80	88.5000	9-23-80	86.4400	800	471108
5	SOYBEANS	11-80	LONG	6-30-80	704.0000	9-26-80	806.0000	5035	476143
1	PORK BELLIES	2-81	LONG	9-4-80	63.1367	9-26-80	64.9411	620	476763
1	PLATINUM	1-81	LONG	8-20-80	691.6000	9-29-80	711.0000	905	477668
1	WORLD SUGAR	3-81	LONG	8-29-80	35.0438	9-29-80	39.7296	5183	482851
1	COMEX SILVER	3-81	LONG	9-4-80	1787.5000	9-29-80	2252.5000	23160	506011
1	COPPER	12-80	LONG	9-11-80	100.5421	9-29-80	93.7490	1763-	504248
1	WORLD SUGAR	3-81	SHORT	9-29-80	39.7296	10-1-80	42.6600	3347-	500901
1	PORK BELLIES	2-81	SHORT	9-26-80	64.9411	10-10-80	69.5262	1807-	499094
1	WORLD SUGAR	3-81	LONG	10-1-80	42.6600	10-15-80	43.3574	716	499810
1	WORLD SUGAR	3-81	SHORT	10-15-80	43.3574	10-17-80	45.2700	2207-	497603
1	WORLD SUGAR	3-81	LONG	10-17-80	45.2700	10-21-80	43.4083	2150-	495453
5	SOYBEANS	11-80	SHORT	9-26-80	806.0000	10-22-80	896.5000	4590-	490863
1	COMEX GOLD	2-81	LONG	9-8-80	711.2000	10-23-80	650.7000	6115-	484748

COMMODITY	DELIV	POSITION	DATE-IN	PRICE-IN	DATE-OUT	PRICE-OUT	NET-PROFIT	CUM-PROFIT
1 JAPANESE YEN	12-80	LONG	8-29-80	.4591	10-27-80	.4695	1235	485983
1 WORLD SUGAR	3-81	SHORT	10-21-80	43.4083	10-30-80	43.5292	200-	485783
5 SOYBEANS	11-80	LONG	10-22-80	896.5000	10-31-80	896.0000	90-	485693
1 WORLD SUGAR	3-81	LONG	10-30-80	43.5292	11- 7-80	42.8200	859-	484834
1 PORK BELLIES	2-81	LONG	10-10-80	69.5262	11-10-80	66.9500	1043-	483791
1 PORK BELLIES	2-81	SHORT	11-10-80	66.9500	11-28-80	72.3218	2106-	481685
1 SOYBEAN MEAL	12-80	LONG	7- 2-80	203.2000	11-28-80	269.3000	6545	488230
1 IMM T-BILLS	12-80	SHORT	7-31-80	91.0300	11-28-80	85.8700	12835	501065
1 COFFEE	12-80	SHORT	9-15-80	130.2600	11-28-80	114.7500	5751	506816
1 JAPANESE YEN	12-80	SHORT	10-27-80	.4695	11-28-80	.4621	860	507676
5 SOYBEANS	7-81	LONG	10-31-80	973.2500	12- 3-80	946.5000	1402-	506274
1 PORK BELLIES	2-81	LONG	11-20-80	72.3218	12- 5-80	67.1558	2028-	504246
1 SOYBEAN MEAL	7-81	LONG	11-28-80	299.2000	12- 5-80	273.5000	2635-	501611
1 HEATING OIL #2	2-81	LONG	9-23-80	86.4400	12- 8-80	94.5700	3349	504960
1 JAPANESE YEN	3-81	SHORT	11-28-80	.4696	12- 8-80	.4918	2840-	502120
1 WORLD SUGAR	3-81	SHORT	11- 7-80	42.8200	12-15-80	29.1517	15243	517363
1 IMM T-BILLS	6-81	SHORT	11-28-80	87.2500	12-19-80	87.4700	615-	516748
1 COFFEE	7-81	LONG	11-28-80	124.4500	12-29-80	130.4600	2318-	514430
1 WORLD SUGAR	3-81	LONG	12-15-80	29.1517	12-29-80	30.7226	1694	516124
1 PLATINUM	1-81	SHORT	9-29-80	711.0000	12-31-80	578.0000	6585	522709
1 HEATING OIL #2	2-81	SHORT	12- 8-80	94.5700	12-31-80	99.1500	1988-	520721

TOTALS FOR THE YEAR 1980:

NET PROFIT FOR YEAR=	412171
EQUITY ON JANUARY 1=	208550
EQUITY ON DECEMBER 31=	620721
PER CENT GAIN ON ORIGINAL EQUITY=	412
TOTAL NUMBER OF TRADES FOR YEAR=	127
NUMBER OF PROFITABLE TRADES FOR YEAR=	61
NUMBER OF LOSING TRADES FOR YEAR=	66
PER CENT PROFITABLE TRADES FOR YEAR=	48
MAXIMUM DRAWDOWN FOR YEAR=	30884-
PROFIT FACTOR FOR YEAR=	3.83
RELATIVE PROFIT FACTOR FOR YEAR=	1.98

86

	COMMODITY	DELIV	POSITION	DATE-IN	PRICE-IN	DATE-OUT	PRICE-OUT	NET-PROFIT	CUM-PROFIT
1	WORLD SUGAR	3-81	SHORT	12-29-80	30.7226	1-5-81	31.9000	1383-	519338
1	WORLD SUGAR	3-81	LONG	1-5-81	31.9000	1-12-81	30.8700	1218-	518120
1	WORLD SUGAR	3-81	SHORT	1-12-81	30.8700	1-23-81	28.7162	2347	520467
1	COFFEE	7-81	LONG	12-29-80	130.4600	1-26-81	125.3500	1981-	518486
1	WORLD SUGAR	3-81	LONG	1-23-81	28.7162	1-29-81	27.4381	1496-	516990
1	COMEX GOLD	2-81	SHORT	10-23-80	650.7000	1-30-81	501.7000	14835	531825
1	PORK BELLIES	2-81	SHORT	12-5-80	67.1558	1-30-81	54.3500	4801	536626
1	WORLD SUGAR	3-81	SHORT	1-29-81	27.4381	1-30-81	26.7900	660	537286
1	HEATING OIL #2	8-81	SHORT	2-5-81	106.8000	2-5-81	106.3000	145	537431
1	IMM T-BILLS	6-81	LONG	12-19-80	87.4700	2-9-81	87.6100	285	537716
1	PLATINUM	7-81	SHORT	12-31-80	630.0000	2-9-81	539.0000	4485	542201
1	PORK BELLIES	7-81	SHORT	1-30-81	59.7250	2-9-81	61.2169	631-	541570
1	WORLD SUGAR	9-81	SHORT	1-30-81	26.9600	2-9-81	28.1600	1409-	540161
1	HEATING OIL #2	8-81	LONG	2-5-81	106.3000	2-9-81	104.3000	905-	539256
1	JAPANESE YEN	3-81	LONG	12-8-80	.4918	2-13-81	.4838	1065-	538191
1	WORLD SUGAR	9-81	LONG	2-9-81	28.1600	2-18-81	24.3000	4388-	533803
1	PORK BELLIES	7-81	LONG	2-9-81	61.2169	2-25-81	58.1193	1242-	532561
1	COPPER	3-81	SHORT	9-29-80	93.7490	2-27-81	80.1500	3334	535895
1	COMEX SILVER	3-81	SHORT	9-29-80	2252.0000	2-27-81	1217.5000	51660	587555
1	JAPANESE YEN	3-81	SHORT	2-13-81	.4838	2-27-81	.4783	622	588177
1	PLATINUM	7-81	LONG	2-9-81	539.0000	3-2-81	461.4000	3945-	584232
1	IMM T-BILLS	6-81	SHORT	2-9-81	87.6100	3-12-81	88.4600	2190-	582042
1	PLATINUM	7-81	SHORT	3-2-81	461.4000	3-16-81	506.7000	2330-	579712
1	COMEX SILVER	9-81	SHORT	2-27-81	1320.0000	3-18-81	1393.0000	3715-	575997
1	COMEX GOLD	8-81	LONG	1-30-81	538.0000	3-20-81	558.4000	2105-	573892
1	PORK BELLIES	7-81	SHORT	2-25-81	58.1193	3-26-81	52.4500	2089	575981
1	COMEX SILVER	9-81	LONG	3-18-81	1393.0000	3-31-81	1266.0000	6415-	569566
1	HEATING OIL #2	8-81	LONG	2-9-81	104.3000	4-6-81	100.2500	1636	571202
1	IMM T-BILLS	6-81	SHORT	3-12-81	88.4600	4-6-81	87.2300	3140-	568062
5	SOYBEANS	7-81	SHORT	12-3-80	946.5000	4-7-81	833.0000	5610	573672
1	SOYBEAN MEAL	7-81	SHORT	12-5-80	273.5000	4-7-81	238.3000	3455	577127
1	PLATINUM	7-81	LONG	3-16-81	506.7000	4-9-81	490.8000	860-	576267
1	COMEX GOLD	8-81	LONG	3-20-81	558.4000	4-13-81	499.4000	5965-	570302
1	HEATING OIL #2	8-81	LONG	4-6-81	100.2500	4-23-81	95.9000	2186-	568116
1	PORK BELLIES	7-81	LONG	3-26-81	52.4500	4-24-81	55.9000	1246	569362
5	SOYBEANS	7-81	LONG	4-7-81	833.0000	5-12-81	760.2500	3702-	565660
1	WORLD SUGAR	9-81	SHORT	2-18-81	24.3000	5-21-81	16.1448	9068	574728
1	PORK BELLIES	7-81	SHORT	4-24-81	55.9000	5-26-81	54.3500	524	575252
1	IMM T-BILLS	6-81	SHORT	4-6-81	87.2300	5-28-81	85.0400	5410	580662
1	JAPANESE YEN	6-81	SHORT	2-27-81	.4878	5-29-81	.4495	4722-	585384
1	IMM T-BILLS	6-81	LONG	5-28-81	85.0400	5-29-81	85.3900	810	586194
1	WORLD SUGAR	9-81	LONG	5-21-81	16.1448	6-4-81	16.9356	820	587014
1	PORK BELLIES	7-81	LONG	5-26-81	54.3500	6-17-81	52.7000	692-	586322
1	SOYBEAN MEAL	7-81	LONG	4-7-81	238.3000	6-24-81	198.9000	4005-	582317
1	COFFEE	7-81	SHORT	1-26-81	125.3500	6-30-81	93.6200	11833	594150
1	PLATINUM	7-81	SHORT	4-9-81	490.8000	6-30-81	404.8000	4235	598385
1	HEATING OIL #2	8-81	SHORT	4-23-81	95.2000	6-30-81	92.0500	1258	599643
5	SOYBEANS	7-81	SHORT	5-12-81	760.2500	6-30-81	686.5000	3622	603265
1	PORK BELLIES	7-81	SHORT	6-17-81	52.7000	6-30-81	45.5000	2671	605936
1	SOYBEAN MEAL	7-81	LONG	6-24-81	198.9000	6-30-81	195.9000	235	606171
1	IMM T-BILLS	12-81	SHORT	5-29-81	87.6000	7-1-81	86.7100	2390-	603781
1	WORLD SUGAR	9-81	SHORT	6-4-81	16.9356	7-10-81	16.6596	244	604025
5	SOYBEANS	11-81	SHORT	6-30-81	731.0000	7-10-81	787.0000	2865-	601160

COMMODITY	DELIV	POSITION	DATE-IN	PRICE-IN	DATE-OUT	PRICE-OUT	NET-PROFIT	CUM-PROFIT
1 HEATING OIL #2	2-82	SHORT	6-30-81	101.2000	7-10-81	103.0000	821-	600339
1 COFFEE	12-81	SHORT	6-30-81	89.0500	7-13-81	95.6000	2521-	597818
1 WORLD SUGAR	9-81	LONG	7-10-81	16.6596	7-20-81	15.6792	1163-	596655
1 COPPER	9-81	SHORT	2-27-81	87.3500	7-31-81	83.5294	890	597545
1 COMEX GOLD	8-81	SHORT	4-13-81	499.4000	7-31-81	403.5000	9525	607070
1 WORLD SUGAR	9-81	SHORT	7-20-81	15.6792	7-31-81	16.7000	1208-	605862
1 COFFEE	12-81	LONG	7-13-81	95.6000	8- 5-81	108.0900	4618	610480
1 PORK BELLIES	2-82	SHORT	6-30-81	63.0000	8- 6-81	66.5766	1424-	609056
1 PLATINUM	1-82	SHORT	6-30-81	438.8000	8-13-81	456.8000	965-	608091
5 SOYBEANS	11-81	LONG	7-10-81	787.0000	8-13-81	694.5000	4690-	603401
1 COMEX SILVER	9-81	SHORT	3-31-81	1266.0000	8-18-81	950.0000	15735	619136
1 COMEX GOLD	2-82	SHORT	7-31-81	433.7000	8-18-81	466.9000	3385-	615751
1 HEATING OIL #2	2-82	LONG	7-10-81	103.0000	8-24-81	101.4700	707-	615044
1 COPPER	9-81	LONG	7-31-81	83.5294	8-25-81	76.8093	1745-	613299
1 PORK BELLIES	2-82	LONG	8- 6-81	66.5766	8-27-81	63.9839	1050-	612249
1 JAPANESE YEN	9-81	SHORT	5-29-81	.4607	8-31-81	.4324	3472	615721
1 COMEX SILVER	9-81	LONG	8-18-81	950.0000	8-31-81	929.5000	1090-	614631
1 COPPER	9-81	SHORT	8-25-81	76.8093	8-31-81	77.4000	212-	614419
1 PORK BELLIES	2-82	SHORT	8-27-81	63.9839	9- 1-81	70.0900	2385-	612034
1 IMM T-BILLS	12-81	SHORT	7- 7-81	86.7100	9-11-81	86.1100	1435	613469
1 COFFEE	12-81	SHORT	8- 5-81	108.0900	9-11-81	115.7506	2937-	610532
1 PORK BELLIES	2-82	LONG	9- 8-81	70.0900	9-23-81	64.5000	2189-	608343
1 WORLD SUGAR	3-82	LONG	7-31-81	16.9800	9-24-81	13.5719	3752	612095
1 PLATINUM	1-82	LONG	8-13-81	456.8000	9-24-81	437.2000	1045-	611050
1 COMEX SILVER	3-82	LONG	8-31-81	1013.2000	9-24-81	1018.0000	175	611225
1 HEATING OIL #2	2-82	SHORT	8-24-81	101.4700	10-15-81	102.6000	539-	610686
1 PORK BELLIES	2-82	SHORT	9-23-81	64.5000	10-19-81	66.6463	880-	609806
1 WORLD SUGAR	3-82	LONG	9-24-81	13.5719	10-19-81	12.0295	1792-	608014
5 SOYBEANS	11-81	SHORT	8-13-81	694.5000	10-30-81	651.5000	2085	610099
1 JAPANESE YEN	12-81	SHORT	8-31-81	.4441	11- 3-81	.4467	390-	609709
1 COMEX GOLD	2-82	LONG	8-18-81	466.9000	11-10-81	422.7000	4485-	605224
1 PORK BELLIES	2-82	LONG	10-19-81	66.6463	11-24-81	65.7825	393-	604831
1 COFFEE	12-81	LONG	9-11-81	115.7500	11-24-81	139.6600	8901	613732
1 WORLD SUGAR	3-82	SHORT	10-19-81	12.0295	11-25-81	12.7107	827-	612905
1 SOYBEAN MEAL	12-81	SHORT	6-30-81	211.2000	11-30-81	187.4000	2315	615220
1 IMM T-BILLS	12-81	LONG	9-11-81	86.1100	11-30-81	89.5300	8485	623705
1 JAPANESE YEN	12-81	LONG	11- 1-81	.4467	11-30-81	.4686	2672	626377
1 COFFEE	12-81	SHORT	11-24-81	139.6600	11-30-81	136.6100	1078	627455
1 HEATING OIL #2	2-82	LONG	10-15-81	102.6000	11-30-81	100.2100	1068-	626387
1 IMM T-BILLS	6-82	LONG	11-30-81	89.1900	12- 9-81	88.1200	2740-	623647
1 PORK BELLIES	2-82	SHORT	11-17-81	65.7825	12-29-81	60.9500	1771	625418
1 PLATINUM	4-82	SHORT	9-24-81	437.2000	12-31-81	373.2000	3135	628553
1 HEATING OIL #2	2-82	SHORT	12- 9-81	100.2100	12-31-81	96.7000	1409	629962

TOTALS FOR THE YEAR 1981:

NET PROFIT FOR YEAR=	109241
EQUITY ON JANUARY 1=	620721
EQUITY ON DECEMBER 31=	729962
PER CENT GAIN ON ORIGINAL EQUITY=	
TOTAL NUMBER OF TRADES FOR YEAR=	96
NUMBER OF PROFITABLE TRADES FOR YEAR=	45
NUMBER OF LOSING TRADES FOR YEAR=	51
PER CENT PROFITABLE TRADES FOR YEAR=	47
MAXIMUM DRAWDOWN FOR YEAR=	22517-
PROFIT FACTOR FOR YEAR=	2.04
RELATIVE PROFIT FACTOR FOR YEAR=	1.06

	COMMODITY	DELIV	POSITION	DATE-IN	PRICE-IN	DATE-OUT	PRICE-OUT	NET-PROFIT	CUM-PROFIT
1	WORLD SUGAR	3-82	LONG	11-25-81	12.7107	1- 4-82	12.7593	10-	629952
1	COFFEE	7-82	SHORT	11-30-81	125.0000	1- 5-82	134.2500	3533-	626419
1	JAPANESE YEN	3-82	LONG	11-30-81	.4747	1-25-82	.4414	4227-	622192
1	WORLD SUGAR	3-82	SHORT	1- 4-82	12.7593	1-25-82	14.0000	1454-	620738
1	COMEX GOLD	2-82	SHORT	11-10-81	422.7000	1-27-82	384.6000	3745	624483
1	PORK BELLIES	2-82	LONG	12-29-81	60.9500	1-29-82	71.8000	4058	628541
1	WORLD SUGAR	3-82	LONG	1-27-82	14.0000	1-29-82	13.5800	535-	628006
1	PORK BELLIES	7-82	LONG	1-29-82	74.4750	1-29-82	69.0422	2129-	625877
1	IMM T-BILLS	6-82	SHORT	12-10-81	88.1200	2-22-82	86.9000	2985	628862
1	WORLD SUGAR	9-82	LONG	1-29-82	14.0800	2-22-82	13.4858	730-	628132
1	PORK BELLIES	7-82	SHORT	2- 9-82	69.0422	2-23-82	73.4323	1733-	626399
1	COPPER	3-82	SHORT	8-31-81	85.1000	2-26-82	69.1500	3922	630321
1	COMEX SILVER	3-82	SHORT	9-24-81	1018.0000	2-26-82	774.3000	12120	642441
1	JAPANESE YEN	3-82	SHORT	1- 5-82	.4414	2-26-82	.4221	2347	644788
1	COFFEE	7-82	LONG	1- 5-82	134.2500	3-16-82	127.2700	2682-	642106
1	HEATING OIL #2	8-82	SHORT	12-31-81	93.0000	3-25-82	75.0000	7495	649601
5	IMM T-BILLS	6-82	LONG	2-22-82	86.9000	3-29-82	86.5800	865-	648736
5	SOYBEANS	7-82	SHORT	10-30-81	729.5000	4- 5-82	671.5000	2835	651571
1	PLATINUM	7-82	SHORT	12-31-81	395.9000	4- 5-82	347.0000	2380	653951
1	COMEX GOLD	8-82	SHORT	1-29-82	409.5000	4- 6-82	375.7000	3315	657266
1	JAPANESE YEN	6-82	SHORT	2-26-82	.4310	4-26-82	.4245	747	658013
1	PLATINUM	6-82	LONG	4- 5-82	347.0000	4-30-82	321.6000	1335-	656678
1	IMM T-BILLS	6-82	SHORT	3-29-82	86.5800	5- 7-82	88.3700	4540-	652138
1	PORK BELLIES	7-82	LONG	2-23-82	73.4323	5-20-82	84.0892	3984	656122
1	COFFEE	7-82	SHORT	3-16-82	127.2700	5-26-82	132.8900	2172-	653950
5	SOYBEANS	7-82	LONG	4- 5-82	671.5000	5-28-82	635.7500	1852-	652098
1	JAPANESE YEN	6-82	SHORT	4-26-82	.4245	5-28-82	.4114	1702	650396
1	IMM T-BILLS	6-82	LONG	5- 7-82	88.3700	5-28-82	88.5700	435	650831
1	JAPANESE YEN	6-82	SHORT	5-28-82	.4114	5-28-82	.4114	65-	650766
1	HEATING OIL #2	8-82	LONG	3-25-82	75.0000	6- 1-82	90.0700	6264	657030
1	HEATING OIL #2	8-82	SHORT	6- 1-82	90.0700	6- 8-82	95.5200	2354-	654676
1	IMM T-BILLS	12-82	LONG	5-28-82	88.0200	6-14-82	86.8500	2990-	651686
1	HEATING OIL #2	8-82	LONG	6- 8-82	95.5200	6-17-82	89.5800	2559-	649127
1	SOYBEAN MEAL	7-82	SHORT	11-30-81	200.9000	6-30-82	178.3000	2195	651322
1	WORLD SUGAR	9-82	SHORT	2-22-82	13.4858	6-30-82	7.8804	6213	657535
1	PLATINUM	7-82	SHORT	4-30-82	321.6000	6-30-82	276.7000	2180	659715
1	PORK BELLIES	7-82	SHORT	5-20-82	84.0892	6-30-82	74.7500	3483	663198
1	COFFEE	7-82	LONG	5-26-82	132.8900	6-30-82	140.6000	2826	666024
5	SOYBEANS	7-82	SHORT	5-28-82	635.7500	6-30-82	610.2500	1210	667234
1	HEATING OIL #2	8-82	SHORT	6-17-82	89.1900	6-30-82	89.1900	98	667332
1	COFFEE	12-82	LONG	6-30-82	127.4600	7- 6-82	118.0200	3605-	663727
1	IMM T-BILLS	12-82	SHORT	6-14-82	86.8500	7- 8-82	87.5800	1890-	661837
1	COMEX SILVER	9-82	SHORT	2-26-82	833.0000	7- 9-82	651.0000	9035	670872
1	PLATINUM	1-83	SHORT	6-30-82	296.4000	7- 9-82	310.2000	755-	670117
1	COPPER	9-82	SHORT	2-26-82	75.0000	7-20-82	67.9982	1685	671802
1	WORLD SUGAR	9-82	LONG	6-30-82	7.8804	7-20-82	7.7843	172-	671630
1	PORK BELLIES	2-83	LONG	6-30-82	73.6750	7-22-82	76.7000	1214-	670416
1	COMEX GOLD	8-82	LONG	4- 6-82	375.7000	7-30-82	342.7000	3365-	667051
1	WORLD SUGAR	9-82	SHORT	7- 6-82	7.7843	7-30-82	7.4900	264	667315
1	COFFEE	12-82	SHORT	6-30-82	118.0200	8- 5-82	122.3200	1677-	665638
1	HEATING OIL #2	2-83	SHORT	6-30-82	91.5000	8- 9-82	94.5000	1325-	664313
1	PLATINUM	1-83	LONG	7- 9-82	310.2000	8- 9-82	273.3000	1910-	662403
1	COPPER	9-82	LONG	7-20-82	67.9982	8- 9-82	59.6000	2164-	660239

	COMMODITY	DELIV	POSITION	DATE-IN	PRICE-IN	DATE-OUT	PRICE-OUT	NET-PROFIT	CUM-PROFIT
1	PORK BELLIES	2-83	LONG	7-22-82	76.7000	8-11-82	73.6366	1229-	659010
1	PORK BELLIES	2-83	SHORT	8-11-82	73.6366	8-13-82	79.4000	2255-	656755
1	PLATINUM	1-83	SHORT	8- 9-82	273.3000	8-19-82	333.6000	3080-	653675
1	JAPANESE YEN	9-82	SHORT	5-28-82	.4188	8-31-82	.3851	4147	657822
1	COMEX SILVER	9-82	LONG	7- 9-82	651.0000	8-31-82	787.0000	6735	664557
1	COPPER	9-82	SHORT	8- 9-82	59.6000	8-31-82	62.5000	790-	663767
1	NYSE COMPOSITE	9-82	LONG	8-23-82	66.8000	8-31-82	68.2000	635	664402
1	PORK BELLIES	2-83	LONG	8-13-82	79.4000	9-14-82	83.6401	1546	665948
1	PLATINUM	1-83	LONG	8-19-82	333.6000	9-20-82	300.4000	1725-	664223
1	COMEX SILVER	3-83	LONG	8-31-82	826.3000	9-27-82	859.0000	1570	665793
1	PORK BELLIES	2-83	SHORT	9-14-82	83.6401	9-27-82	88.9000	2063-	663730
1	COMEX GOLD	2-83	LONG	7-30-82	362.9000	9-29-82	407.0000	4345	668075
1	PORK BELLIES	2-83	LONG	9-27-82	88.9000	10- 1-82	82.3292	2561-	665514
1	PLATINUM	1-83	SHORT	9-20-82	300.4000	10-11-82	351.3000	2610-	662904
1	COMEX SILVER	3-83	SHORT	9-27-82	859.0000	10-11-82	984.5000	6340-	656564
1	COMEX GOLD	2-83	SHORT	9-29-82	407.0000	10-13-82	466.7000	6035-	650529
1	COPPER	3-83	SHORT	8-31-82	66.1000	10-14-82	69.8563	1004-	649525
1	HEATING OIL #2	2-83	LONG	8- 9-82	94.5000	10-27-82	97.2700	1098	650623
5	SOYBEANS	11-82	SHORT	6-30-82	624.5000	10-29-82	533.2500	4497	655120
1	WORLD SUGAR	3-83	SHORT	7-30-82	8.7800	10-29-82	7.7086	1134	656254
1	COFFEE	12-82	LONG	8- 5-82	122.3200	11- 1-82	135.0200	4697	660951
1	SOYBEAN MEAL	12-82	SHORT	6-30-82	184.5000	11- 5-82	172.5000	1125	662076
1	COMEX SILVER	3-83	LONG	10-11-82	984.5000	11-11-82	973.8000	600-	661476
1	PORK BELLIES	2-83	SHORT	10- 1-82	82.3292	11-12-82	82.2557	37-	661439
1	JAPANESE YEN	12-82	LONG	8-31-82	.3892	11-16-82	.3813	922	662361
1	PORK BELLIES	2-83	LONG	11-12-82	82.2557	11-26-82	78.4416	1514-	660847
1	IMM T-BILLS	12-82	LONG	7- 8-82	87.5800	11-30-82	91.7500	10360	671207
1	NYSE COMPOSITE	12-82	LONG	8-31-82	68.4500	11-30-82	81.6500	6535	677742
1	COFFEE	12-82	SHORT	11- 1-82	135.0200	11-30-82	136.6500	676-	677066
1	SOYBEAN MEAL	12-82	LONG	11- 5-82	172.5000	11-30-82	175.4000	225	677291
1	JAPANESE YEN	12-82	LONG	11-16-82	.3813	11-30-82	.4018	2497	679788
1	COMEX SILVER	3-83	SHORT	11-11-82	973.8000	12- 2-82	1066.0000	4675-	675113
1	HEATING OIL #2	2-83	SHORT	10-27-82	97.2700	12- 9-82	88.3600	3677	678790
1	WORLD SUGAR	3-83	LONG	10-29-82	7.7086	12- 9-82	7.0800	769-	678021
1	HEATING OIL #2	2-83	LONG	12- 9-82	88.3600	12-21-82	82.6800	2450-	675571
1	PLATINUM	1-83	LONG	10-11-82	351.3000	12-30-82	383.1000	1525	677096
1	HEATING OIL #2	2-83	SHORT	12-21-82	82.6800	12-30-82	84.3100	749-	676347

TOTALS FOR THE YEAR 1982:

```
NET PROFIT FOR YEAR=                          46385
EQUITY ON JANUARY 1=                         729962
EQUITY ON DECEMBER 31=                       776347
PER CENT GAIN ON ORIGINAL EQUITY=                46
TOTAL NUMBER OF TRADES FOR YEAR=                 90
NUMBER OF PROFITABLE TRADES FOR YEAR=            42
NUMBER OF LOSING TRADES FOR YEAR=                48
PER CENT PROFITABLE TRADES FOR YEAR=             47
MAXIMUM DRAWDOWN FOR YEAR=                    22277-
PROFIT FACTOR FOR YEAR=                        1.47
RELATIVE PROFIT FACTOR FOR YEAR=               0.77
```

	COMMODITY	DELIV	POSITION	DATE-IN	PRICE-IN	DATE-OUT	PRICE-OUT	NET-PROFIT	CUM-PROFIT
1	PORK BELLIES	2-83	SHORT	11-26-82	78.4416	1-14-83	86.3250	3060-	673287
1	JAPANESE YEN	3-83	LONG	11-30-82	.4047	1-14-83	.4193	1760	675047
1	PORK BELLIES	2-83	LONG	1-14-83	86.3250	1-24-83	81.6922	1825-	673222
1	COMEX GOLD	2-83	LONG	10-13-82	466.7000	1-28-83	510.1000	4275	677497
1	WORLD SUGAR	3-83	SHORT	12-9-82	7.0800	1-31-83	6.2000	920	678417
1	PORK BELLIES	2-83	SHORT	1-28-83	81.6922	1-31-83	80.4750	397	678814
1	WORLD SUGAR	9-83	SHORT	1-31-83	7.3400	1-31-83	7.9457	743-	678071
1	PLATINUM	1-84	SHORT	2-2-83	482.5000	2-11-83	458.1000	1155	679226
1	COMEX SILVER	3-83	LONG	12-2-82	1066.0000	2-22-83	1356.0000	14435	693661
1	PLATINUM	7-83	LONG	12-30-82	400.1000	2-23-83	443.6000	2110	695771
1	COMEX GOLD	8-83	LONG	1-31-83	534.6000	2-23-83	485.8000	4945-	690826
1	PLATINUM	1-84	LONG	2-22-83	458.1000	2-25-83	445.8000	680-	690146
1	COPPER	3-83	LONG	10-14-82	69.8563	2-28-83	73.6500	883	691029
1	SOYBEAN MEAL	7-83	LONG	11-30-82	179.2000	2-28-83	174.6000	525-	690504
1	NYSE COMPOSITE	3-83	LONG	11-30-82	82.3500	2-28-83	86.2000	1860	692364
1	JAPANESE YEN	3-83	SHORT	1-24-83	.4193	2-28-83	.4178	122	692486
1	WORLD SUGAR	9-83	LONG	2-11-83	7.9457	2-28-83	6.8700	1269-	691217
1	COMEX SILVER	3-83	SHORT	2-23-83	1356.0000	2-28-83	1030.0000	16235	707452
1	COPPER	9-83	LONG	1-6-83	78.0000	3-4-83	75.6101	662-	706790
1	HEATING OIL #2	8-83	SHORT	2-25-83	575.2500	3-15-83	650.7500	1875	708665
5	SOYBEANS	7-83	SHORT	10-29-82	575.2500	3-23-83	650.7500	3840-	704825
1	SOYBEAN MEAL	7-83	SHORT	2-28-83	174.6030	3-23-83	195.6000	2165-	702660
1	WORLD SUGAR	9-83	SHORT	2-23-83	6.8700	4-4-83	7.8779	1193-	701467
1	PLATINUM	7-83	SHORT	2-28-83	443.6000	4-14-83	432.8000	475	701942
1	COMEX SILVER	9-83	SHORT	3-15-83	1232.6000	4-14-83	1229.0000	115	702057
1	HEATING OIL #2	8-83	LONG	2-25-83	73.6800	4-18-83	79.4700	2366	704423
1	PLATINUM	1-84	SHORT	2-28-83	445.8000	5-11-83	456.1000	580-	703843
1	JAPANESE YEN	6-83	SHORT	11-30-82	.4202	5-16-83	.4346	1865-	701978
1	COFFEE	7-83	SHORT	11-30-82	128.0600	5-31-83	129.4800	597-	701381
1	IMM T-BILLS	6-83	LONG	2-28-83	90.6100	5-31-83	91.3000	1660	703041
1	NYSE COMPOSITE	6-83	LONG	4-14-83	86.8500	5-31-83	94.3000	3660	706701
1	JAPANESE YEN	9-83	LONG	5-11-83	.4346	6-1-83	.4177	2177-	704524
1	COMEX SILVER	9-83	LONG	4-18-83	1229.0000	6-1-83	1280.8000	2525	707049
1	PLATINUM	1-84	LONG	4-4-83	456.1000	6-2-83	432.7000	1235-	705814
1	WORLD SUGAR	9-83	SHORT	6-2-83	11.0634	6-23-83	7.8779	3502	709316
1	WORLD SUGAR	9-83	LONG	3-23-83	11.1054	6-29-83	10.2140	763-	708553
5	SOYBEANS	7-83	SHORT	1-31-83	650.7500	6-30-83	576.0000	3802	704751
1	PORK BELLIES	7-83	SHORT	3-23-83	78.8250	6-30-83	60.8500	6765	711516
1	SOYBEAN MEAL	7-83	LONG	5-16-83	195.6000	6-30-83	176.9000	1935-	709581
1	COFFEE	7-83	LONG	6-29-83	129.4800	6-30-83	124.6300	1883-	707698
5	SOYBEANS	7-83	SHORT	6-30-83	576.0000	7-11-83	606.0000	1565-	706133
5	SOYBEANS	11-83	SHORT	6-23-83	628.2500	7-15-83	667.5000	2027-	704106
1	WORLD SUGAR	9-83	SHORT	6-30-83	11.6869	7-21-83	10.2140	1714-	702392
1	PORK BELLIES	2-84	SHORT	7-15-83	55.9000	7-22-83	59.0250	1252-	701140
1	WORLD SUGAR	8-83	SHORT	2-23-83	10.2140	7-29-83	11.1054	1063-	700077
1	COMEX GOLD	9-83	SHORT	2-23-83	485.8000	7-29-83	412.8000	7235	707312
1	WORLD SUGAR	12-83	LONG	7-22-83	11.1054	8-30-83	11.2900	141	707453
1	SOYBEAN MEAL	9-83	LONG	6-30-83	185.2000	8-31-83	234.3000	4845	712298
1	COFFEE	9-83	SHORT	5-31-83	75.6101	8-31-83	71.6500	925	713223
1	JAPANESE YEN	9-83	LONG	5-31-83	.4213	8-31-83	.4073	1815-	711408
1	NYSE COMPOSITE	9-83	LONG	6-1-83	95.0500	8-31-83	95.1500	15-	711393
1	COMEX SILVER	9-83	SHORT	5-31-83	1280.8000	8-31-83	1210.0000	3475	714868
1	HEATING OIL #2	2-84	LONG	8-4-83	88.4600	8-31-83	85.3500	1371-	713497

	COMMODITY	DELIV	POSITION	DATE-IN	PRICE-IN	DATE-OUT	PRICE-OUT	NET-PROFIT	CUM-PROFIT
1	WORLD SUGAR	3-84	LONG	7-29-83	12.7900	9-14-83	11.0482	2015-	711482
5	SOYBEANS	11-83	LONG	7-11-83	667.5000	9-15-83	857.5000	9435	720917
1	PORK BELLIES	2-84	LONG	7-21-83	59.0250	9-21-83	59.2500	20	720937
1	WORLD SUGAR	3-84	SHORT	9-14-83	11.0482	10- 6-83	11.7647	867-	720070
1	PORK BELLIES	2-84	SHORT	9-21-83	59.2500	10-17-83	60.9200	699-	719371
1	WORLD SUGAR	3-84	LONG	10- 6-83	11.7647	10-20-83	10.5988	1370-	718001
5	SOYBEANS	11-83	SHORT	9-15-83	857.5000	10-31-83	812.0000	2210	720211
1	COMEX SILVER	3-84	SHORT	8-31-83	1274.8000	11-29-83	966.0000	15375	735586
1	IMM T-BILLS	12-83	LONG	5-31-83	90.7300	11-30-83	91.0700	785	736371
1	COFFEE	12-83	LONG	6-30-83	125.1900	11-30-83	150.7800	9531	745902
1	SOYBEAN MEAL	12-83	SHORT	8-30-83	234.3000	11-30-83	223.2000	1045	746947
1	JAPANESE YEN	12-83	LONG	8-31-83	.4111	11-30-83	.4312	2447	749394
1	NYSE COMPOSITE	12-83	LONG	8-31-83	95.8000	11-30-83	96.3000	185	749579
1	COMEX SILVER	3-84	LONG	11-29-83	966.0000	12-16-83	877.0000	4515-	745064
1	HEATING OIL #2	2-84	SHORT	8-31-83	85.3500	12-23-83	81.7300	1455	746519
5	SOYBEANS	7-84	SHORT	10-31-83	846.5000	12-27-83	854.5000	490-	746029
1	PLATINUM	1-84	SHORT	6- 1-83	432.7000	12-30-83	390.5000	2045	748074
1	HEATING OIL #2	2-84	LONG	12-23-83	81.7300	12-30-83	82.6500	321	748395

TOTALS FOR THE YEAR 1983:

```
NET PROFIT FOR YEAR=                    72048
EQUITY ON JANUARY 1=                   776347
EQUITY ON DECEMBER 31=                 848395
PER CENT GAIN ON ORIGINAL EQUITY=          72
TOTAL NUMBER OF TRADES FOR YEAR=           71
NUMBER OF PROFITABLE TRADES FOR YEAR=      37
NUMBER OF LOSING TRADES FOR YEAR=          34
PER CENT PROFITABLE TRADES FOR YEAR=       52
MAXIMUM ...  N FOR YEAR=                11439-
PROFIT FACTOR FOR YEAR=                  2.27
RELATIVE PROFIT FACTOR FOR YEAR=         1.08
```

92

COMMODITY	DELIV	POSITION	DATE-IN	PRICE-IN	DATE-OUT	PRICE-OUT	NET-PROFIT	CUM-PROFIT
1 PORK BELLIES	2-84	LONG	10-17-83	60.9200	1- 3-84	60.7056	146-	748249
1 PORK BELLIES	2-84	SHORT	1- 3-84	60.7056	1-13-84	66.4759	2257-	745992
5 SOYBEANS	7-84	LONG	12-27-83	854.5000	1-17-84	765.7500	4502-	741490
1 COMEX GOLD	2-84	SHORT	7-29-83	435.3000	1-31-84	373.8000	6085	747575
1 WORLD SUGAR	3-84	SHORT	10-20-83	10.5988	1-31-84	7.5000	3405	750980
1 PORK BELLIES	2-84	LONG	1-13-84	66.4759	1-31-84	65.5000	435-	750545
1 COMEX SILVER	3-84	SHORT	12-16-83	877.0000	2- 1-84	886.0000	515-	750030
1 COFFEE	7-84	LONG	11-30-83	136.0000	2- 7-84	130.7900	2018-	748012
1 NYSE COMPOSITE	3-84	LONG	11-30-83	97.5000	2- 8-84	90.3000	3665-	744347
1 PORK BELLIES	7-84	LONG	1-31-84	68.4750	2-13-84	65.1500	1328-	743019
1 COPPER	3-84	SHORT	8-31-83	76.1000	2-29-84	64.9500	2722	745741
1 JAPANESE YEN	3-84	LONG	11-30-83	.4347	2-29-84	.4292	752-	744989
1 COMEX SILVER	3-84	LONG	2- 1-84	886.0000	2-29-84	966.0000	3935	748924
1 NYSE COMPOSITE	3-84	SHORT	2- 8-84	90.3000	2-29-84	90.6000	215-	748709
1 SOYBEAN MEAL	7-84	SHORT	11-30-83	225.5000	3- 5-84	210.4000	1445	750154
1 SOYBEANS	7-84	SHORT	1-17-84	765.5000	3- 5-84	795.5000	1552-	748602
1 PORK BELLIES	7-84	SHORT	2-13-84	65.1500	3- 9-84	66.6529	636-	747966
1 SOYBEAN MEAL	7-84	LONG	2-13-84	210.4000	4-11-84	199.1000	1195-	746771
1 PORK BELLIES	7-84	LONG	3- 2-84	66.6529	4-18-84	68.1000	484	747255
1 COMEX SILVER	9-84	LONG	3- 9-84	1015.0000	5-11-84	892.3000	6225-	741030
1 COFFEE	7-84	SHORT	2-29-84	130.7900	5-11-84	151.7400	7921-	733109
1 JAPANESE YEN	6-84	LONG	2-29-84	.4332	5-18-84	.4304	415-	732694
1 COFFEE	7-84	LONG	5-11-84	151.7400	5-25-84	145.0600	2570-	730124
1 IMM T-BILLS	6-84	LONG	11-30-83	90.3900	5-31-84	90.1800	590-	729534
1 NYSE COMPOSITE	6-84	SHORT	2-29-84	91.7000	5-31-84	87.0500	2260	731794
1 JAPANESE YEN	6-84	SHORT	5-18-84	.4304	5-31-84	.4328	365-	731429
5 SOYBEANS	7-84	LONG	3- 5-84	795.5000	6- 1-84	826.5000	1485	732914
1 HEATING OIL #2	8-84	LONG	4-23-84	79.3000	6- 8-84	79.6700	90	733004
1 PORK BELLIES	7-84	SHORT	4-18-84	68.1000	6-12-84	68.9294	380-	732624
1 PORK BELLIES	7-84	LONG	6-12-84	68.9294	6-26-84	66.3500	1045-	731579
1 COFFEE	7-84	SHORT	5-25-84	145.0600	6-27-84	152.7500	2948-	728631
1 SOYBEAN MEAL	7-84	SHORT	4-11-84	199.1000	6-29-84	177.0000	2145	730776
5 SOYBEANS	7-84	SHORT	6- 1-84	826.5000	6-29-84	747.5000	3872	734648
1 HEATING OIL #2	8-84	SHORT	6- 8-84	79.6700	6-29-84	77.9500	657	735305
1 PORK BELLIES	7-84	SHORT	6-26-84	66.3500	6-29-84	62.7000	1322	736627
1 COFFEE	7-84	LONG	6-27-84	152.7500	6-29-84	149.5000	1283-	735344
1 COFFEE	12-84	LONG	6-29-84	140.3500	6-29-84	137.0600	1298-	734046
1 JAPANESE YEN	6-85	SHORT	7- 2-84	.4290	7-11-84	.4310	315-	733731
1 WORLD SUGAR	9-84	SHORT	6-29-84	8.4000	7-11-84	4.4000	4415	738146
1 COMEX GOLD	8-84	SHORT	1-31-84	391.6000	7-31-84	337.7000	5325	743471
1 NYSE COMPOSITE	9-84	SHORT	5-31-84	88.3000	7-31-84	94.7500	3290-	740181
1 COFFEE	12-84	SHORT	7-11-84	137.0600	8- 3-84	142.2900	2026-	738155
1 HEATING OIL #2	12-85	SHORT	7-11-84	81.8500	8-21-84	82.0000	128-	738027
1 WORLD SUGAR	3-85	SHORT	7-31-84	5.7200	8-28-84	5.9800	356-	737671
1 COPPER	9-84	SHORT	2-29-84	68.7500	8-31-84	61.1500	1835	739506
1 COMEX SILVER	9-84	SHORT	5- 7-84	892.3000	8-31-84	745.2000	7290	746796
1 JAPANESE YEN	9-84	SHORT	5-31-84	.4389	8-31-84	.4143	3010	749806
1 NYSE COMPOSITE	9-84	LONG	8- 3-84	94.7500	8-31-84	96.7000	910	750716
1 COFFEE	12-84	LONG	8-10-84	142.2900	9-12-84	139.6100	1070-	749646
1 JAPANESE YEN	6-85	LONG	7-23-84	.4310	9-17-84	.4200	1440-	748206
1 WORLD SUGAR	3-85	LONG	8-28-84	5.9800	9-17-84	5.1230	1024-	747182
1 WORLD SUGAR	3-85	SHORT	9-17-84	5.1230	10- 3-84	5.9900	1036-	746146
1 PORK BELLIES	2-85	SHORT	6-29-84	77.0250	10- 4-84	65.6429	4260	750406

	COMMODITY	DELIV	POSITION	DATE-IN	PRICE-IN	DATE-OUT	PRICE-OUT	NET-PROFIT	CUM-PROFIT
1	HEATING OIL #2	2-85	LONG	8-21-84	82.0000	10-12-84	80.5803	661-	749745
5	SOYBEANS	11-84	SHORT	6-29-84	728.0000	10-15-84	632.7500	4697	754442
1	PORK BELLIES	2-85	LONG	10- 4-84	65.6429	10-19-84	62.0139	1444-	752998
5	SOYBEANS	11-84	LONG	10-15-84	632.7500	10-19-84	619.0000	752-	752246
1	PORK BELLIES	2-85	SHORT	10-19-84	62.0139	10-31-84	67.0023	1960-	750286
1	COFFEE	12-84	SHORT	9-12-84	139.6100	11-12-84	143.5400	1538-	748748
1	WORLD SUGAR	3-85	LONG	10- 3-84	5.9900	11-19-84	5.2894	849-	747899
1	IMM T-BILLS	12-84	LONG	5-31-84	87.8400	11-30-84	91.5400	9185	757084
1	SOYBEAN MEAL	12-84	SHORT	6-29-84	190.2000	11-30-84	150.2000	3935	761019
1	JAPANESE YEN	12-84	SHORT	8-31-84	.4201	11-30-84	.4043	1910	762929
1	NYSE COMPOSITE	12-84	LONG	8-31-84	98.3000	11-30-84	94.9000	1765-	761164
1	COFFEE	12-84	LONG	11-12-84	143.5400	11-30-84	138.8600	1820-	759344
1	PORK BELLIES	2-85	LONG	10-31-84	67.0023	12-10-84	70.5511	1283	760627
1	PORK BELLIES	2-85	SHORT	12-10-84	70.5511	12-26-84	77.5800	2735-	757892
1	HEATING OIL #2	2-85	SHORT	10-12-84	80.5800	12-28-84	73.3200	2984	760876

TOTALS FOR THE YEAR 1984:

```
NET PROFIT FOR YEAR=                      12481
EQUITY ON JANUARY 1=                     848395
EQUITY ON DECEMBER 31=                   860876
PER CENT GAIN ON ORIGINAL EQUITY=            12
TOTAL NUMBER OF TRADES FOR YEAR=             68
NUMBER OF PROFITABLE TRADES FOR YEAR=        26
NUMBER OF LOSING TRADES FOR YEAR=            42
PER CENT PROFITABLE TRADES FOR YEAR=         38
MAXIMUM DRAWDOWN FOR YEAR=                22349-
PROFIT FACTOR FOR YEAR=                    1.18
RELATIVE PROFIT FACTOR FOR YEAR=           0.72
```

94

COMMODITY	DELIV	POSITION	DATE-IN	PRICE-IN	DATE-OUT	PRICE-OUT	NET-PROFIT	CUM-PROFIT
5 SOYBEANS	7-85	LONG	10-31-84	667.5000	1- 4-85	595.2500	3677-	757199
1 WORLD SUGAR	3-85	SHORT	11-19-84	5.2894	1-14-85	4.8378	440	757639
1 PORK BELLIES	2-85	LONG	12-26-84	77.5800	1-16-85	71.9852	2191-	755448
1 COMEX GOLD	2-85	SHORT	7-31-84	357.3000	1-31-85	304.1000	5255	760703
1 WORLD SUGAR	3-85	LONG	1-14-85	4.8378	1-31-85	4.3200	644-	760059
1 PORK BELLIES	2-85	SHORT	1-16-85	71.9852	1-31-85	71.2500	214	760273
1 COPPER	3-85	SHORT	8-31-84	64.9500	2-28-85	58.6500	1510	761783
1 COMEX SILVER	3-85	SHORT	8-31-84	788.7000	2-28-85	562.5000	11245	773028
1 JAPANESE YEN	6-85	SHORT	9-17-84	.4200	2-28-85	.3886	3860	776888
1 JAPANESE YEN	3-85	SHORT	11-30-84	.4074	2-28-85	.3853	2697	779585
1 NYSE COMPOSITE	3-85	LONG	11-30-84	96.3500	2-28-85	105.4500	4485	784070
1 IMM T-BILLS	6-85	LONG	11-30-84	90.7000	3- 1-85	90.6700	140-	783930
1 PORK BELLIES	7-85	SHORT	1-31-85	73.2250	3- 6-85	73.4746	159-	783771
1 PORK BELLIES	7-85	LONG	3- 6-85	73.4746	4- 1-85	70.8616	1057-	782714
1 COFFEE	7-85	LONG	12- 3-84	134.7600	4-12-85	139.2900	1633	784347
1 IMM T-BILLS	6-85	SHORT	3- 1-85	90.6700	4-16-85	92.0600	3540-	780807
1 COFFEE	7-85	SHORT	4-12-85	139.2900	4-24-85	146.6900	2840-	777967
1 SOYBEAN MEAL	7-85	SHORT	11-30-84	169.7000	4-26-85	129.2000	3985	781952
5 SOYBEANS	7-85	SHORT	1- 4-85	595.2500	4-26-85	604.2500	515-	781437
1 NYSE COMPOSITE	6-85	LONG	2-28-85	107.9500	4-26-85	106.3500	865-	780572
1 PORK BELLIES	7-85	SHORT	4- 1-85	65.8750	4-26-85	65.8750	1829	782401
1 IMM T-BILLS	6-85	LONG	4-16-85	92.0600	4-26-85	92.0300	140-	782261
1 COFFEE	7-85	LONG	4-24-85	146.6900	4-26-85	146.4800	143-	782118

TOTALS FOR THE YEAR 1985 THROUGH APRIL26:

```
NET PROFIT FOR YEAR=                          21242
EQUITY ON JANUARY 1=                         860876
EQUITY ON APRIL 26                           882118
PER CENT GAIN ON ORIGINAL EQUITY=                21
TOTAL NUMBER OF TRADES FOR YEAR=                 23
NUMBER OF PROFITABLE TRADES FOR YEAR=            11
NUMBER OF LOSING TRADES FOR YEAR=                12
PER CENT PROFITABLE TRADES FOR YEAR=             48
MAXIMUM DRAWDOWN FOR YEAR=                     6380-
PROFIT FACTOR FOR YEAR=                        2.33
RELATIVE PROFIT FACTOR FOR YEAR=               1.19
```

95

TOTALS FOR ALL CONTRACTS OF ALL COMMODITIES:

INITIAL EQUITY=	100000
NET PROFIT=	782118
PER CENT GAIN ON INITIAL EQUITY=	782
TOTAL NUMBER OF TRADES=	585
NUMBER OF PROFITABLE TRADES=	276
NUMBER OF LOSING TRADES=	309
PER CENT PROFITABLE TRADES=	47
PROFITABLE TRADES TOTAL=	1357626
LOSING TRADES TOTAL=	575508-
AVERAGE PROFITABLE TRADE=	4918
AVERAGE LOSING TRADE=	1862-
RATIO OF AVERAGE PROFITABLE TRADE TO AVERAGE LOSING ONE=	2.64
MAXIMUM DRAWDOWN=	30884-
AVERAGE PROFIT PER TRADE=	1336
RELATIVE PROFIT FACTOR=	1.24
PROFIT FACTOR=	2.35
SHARPE RATIO=	1.02

NOTE: $65.00 DAY AND $65.00 OVERNIGHT BROKERAGE COMMISSIONS
      HAVE BEEN DEDUCTED FROM EACH WINNING TRADE AND
      ADDED TO EACH LOSING TRADE.

The Maxtrend System
Suggested Portfolios
And Their Historical Performance

$10,000 PORTFOLIO

Portfolio I.   **(General Diversification)**

    1 Gold
    1 Soybean
    1 Sugar
    1 T-Bill

Approximate Margin Required*:	$ 4,800
Total 7-Year Net Profit:	$168,635
Total No. Trades:	187
Avg. Net Profit/Trade:	$ 901

Portfolio II.   **(General Diversification)**

    1 Coffee
    1 Japanese Yen
    1 Pork Belly
    1 T-Bill

Approximate Margin Required:	$ 5,000
Total 7-Year Net Profit:	$136,198
Total No. Trades:	234
Avg. Net Profit/Trade:	$ 582

---

* Margin subject to change without notice. But, the margin totals shown here, generally, are close to what normally can be expected.

Portfolio III.   (Metals Only)

    1 Copper
    1 Gold
    1 Platinum
    1 Silver

Approximate Margin Required:	$ 5,000
Total 7-Year Net Profit:	$559,204
Total No. Trades:	143
Avg. Net Profit/Trade:	$ 3,910

Portfolio IV.   (Financials & Currencies Only)

    2 Japanese Yen
    2 T-Bills

Approximate Margin Required:	$ 5,000
Total 7-Year Net Profit:	$159,346
Total No. Trades:	178
Avg. Net Profit/Trade:	$ 895

Portfolio V.   (Internationals)

    1 Coffee
    1 Gold
    1 Heating Oil
    1 Sugar

Approximate Margin Required:	$ 4,800
Total 7-Year Net Profit:	$168,702
Total No. Trades:	208
Avg. Net Profit/Trade:	$ 812

$25,000 PORTFOLIO

Portfolio VI.   **(General Diversification)**

   1 Coffee
   1 Gold
   1 Japanese Yen
   1 NYSE Composite
   1 Pork Belly
   1 Soybean
   1 Sugar
   1 T-Bill

Approximate Margin Required: $ 12,500
Total 7-Year Net Profit: $270,548
Total Number Trades: 400
Avg. Net Profit/Trade: $ 676

Portfolio VII.   **(General Diversification)**

   2 Coffee
   3 Japanese Yen
   1 Silver
   4 Soybean Meal
   2 T-Bills

Approximate Margin Required: $ 14,000
Total 7-Year Net Profit: $799,244
Total No. Trades: 505
Avg. Net Profit/Trade: $ 1,582

Portfolio VIII.   **(Metals Only)**

   4 Copper
   2 Gold
   3 Platinum
   1 Silver

Approximate Margin Required: $ 11,500
Total 7-Year Net Profit: $590,816
Total No. Trades: 354
Avg. Net Profit/Trade: $ 1,668

Portfolio IX.   (Financials & Currencies Only)

    5 Japanese Yen
    5 T-Bills

Approximate Margin Required:	$ 12,500
Total 7-Year Net Profit:	$398,365
Total Number Trades:	445
Avg. Net Profit/Trade:	$ 895

Portfolio X.   (Internationals)

    2 Coffee
    1 Gold
    4 Heating Oil
    3 Sugar

Approximate Margin Required:	$ 11,500
Total 7-Year Net Profit:	$311,047
Total Number Trades:	555
Avg. Net Profit/Trade:	$ 560

$50,000 PORTFOLIO

Portfolio XI.   (General Diversification)

    1 Coffee
    1 Copper
    1 Gold
    1 Heating Oil
    1 Japanese Yen
    1 NYSE Composite
    1 Platinum
    1 Pork Belly
    1 Silver
    1 Soybean
    1 Soybean Meal
    1 Sugar
    1 T-Bill

Approximate Margin Required:	$ 20,000
Total 7-Year Net Profit:	$782,088
Total Number Trades:	585
Avg. Net Profit/Trade:	$ 1,336

Portfolio XII.   **(General Diversification)**

    2 Coffee
    1 Gold
    3 Japanese Yen
    3 Platinum
    1 Silver
    4 Soybean Meal
    3 Sugar
    2 T-Bills

Approximate Margin Required:	$ 22,000
Total 7-Year Net Profit:	$1,056,362
Total Number Trades:	937
Avg. Net Profit/Trade:	$ 1,127

Portfolio XIII.   **(Metals Only)**

    8 Copper
    4 Gold
    6 Platinum
    2 Silver

Approximate Margin Required:	$ 23,000
Total 7-Year Net Profit:	$1,503,632
Total Number Trades:	708
Avg. Net Profit/Trade:	$ 2,123

Portfolio XIV.   **(Financials & Currencies Only)**

    9 Japanese Yen
    7 T-Bills

Approximate Margin Required:	$ 21,000
Total 7-Year Net Profit:	$ 627,057
Total Number Trades:	731
Avg. Net Profit/Trade:	$ 857

Portfolio XV.   (Internationals)

4 Coffee
4 Gold
4 Heating Oil
4 Sugar

Approximate Margin Required:	$ 20,000
Total 7-Year Net Profit:	$674,808
Total Number of Trades:	832
Avg. Net Profit/Trade:	$ 811

$100,000 PORTFOLIO

Portfolio XVI.   (General Diversification—All Commodities With Risk Distribution)

2 Coffee
3 Copper
1 Gold
5 Heating Oil
2 Japanese Yen
2 NYSE Composite
2 Platinum
9 Pork Bellies
1 Silver
4 Soybeans
2 Soybean Meal
5 Sugars
1 T-Bill

Approximate Margin Required:	$ 48,000
Total 7-Year Net Profit:	$1,246,644
Total Number Trades:	2,076
Avg. Net Profit/Trade:	$ 600

Portfolio XVII   (Medium Risk/Medium Reward)

8 Coffee
4 Gold
10 Japanese Yen
10 Platinum
2 Silver
7 T-Bills

Approximate Margin Required:	$ 49,000
Total 7-Year Net Profit:	$2,521,150
Total Number Trades:	1,897
Avg. Net Profit/Trade:	$ 1,329

Portfolio XVIII   (High Risk/High Reward)

16 Coffee
8 Gold
4 Silver
12 T-Bills

Approximate Margin Required:	$ 54,000
Total 7-Year Net Profit:	$3,656,340
Total Number Trades:	1,704
Avg. Net Profit/Trade:	$ 2,145

Note: A $65.00 commission has been charged to all trades.

Sample Work Sheets
& Trade Records

Work Sheet & Trade Record

Contract Month & Year __JULY '80__ Commodity __COPPER__ Page __1__

'79 DATE AUGUST	HIGH	LOW	CLOSE	DPA	ARO	ADAR	ARVF	PDR	PDVF	CVF	CF	TI	TI PDR (RATIO)	EF	ADD OR SUB. TO TI	ORDER GO LONG OR SHORT AT >MTN	TRADE ACTION & ACT. FLL	TRADE PROFIT OR LOSS
1	86.10	84.00	85.65	85.25	—													
2	87.00	85.30	87.00	86.43	1.70													
3	87.70	86.00	86.00	86.57	1.70													
6	86.35	84.80	86.35	85.83	1.55													
7	87.25	86.20	86.70	86.78	.90													
8	86.65	87.10	86.65	87.23	1.35													
9	89.20	87.40	87.30	87.67	1.90													
10	89.50	88.30	89.45	89.12	.80													
13	88.05	87.90	88.35	88.32	1.25													
14	91.35	89.80	91.25	90.73	3.00													
15	91.40	90.50	90.45	90.85	.90													
16	90.75	89.65	89.85	90.06	1.70													
17	90.30	88.85	89.95	89.95	1.65													
20	90.30	88.75	89.25	88.92	2.05													
21	90.00	88.55	90.00	89.52	1.75													
22	90.50	88.90	89.25	89.23	1.90	1.50												
23	90.50	88.65	90.25	89.80	1.90	1.53	7	6.60	4	6	.105	89.18	89.18 27/8	4.65	+1	↓S 93.85	/	/
24	92.30	91.10	91.75	91.75	2.05	1.56	7	7.50	5	6	.105	89.25	89.25 27/8	4.65	+1	↓S 93.86 .63	/	/

F.T.C.

Work Sheet & Trade Record

DATE	HIGH	LOW	CLOSE	DPA	ARO	ADAR	ARVF	PDR	PDVF	CVF	CF	TI	PDR (DATE)	EF	ADD OR SUB. TO TI	ORDER GO LONG OR SHORT	AT >MTN	TRADE ACTION & ACT. FLL	TRADE PROFIT OR LOSS

Work Sheet & Trade Record

Contract Month & Year _____ Commodity _____ Page _____

DATE	HIGH	LOW	CLOSE	DPA	AIRO	ADAR	ARYF	PDR	PDVF	CYF	CF	TI	PDR (RATE)	EF	ADD OR SUB. TO TI	ORDER GO LONG OR SHORT AT > MTN	TRADE ACTION & ACT. FILL	TRADE PROFIT OR LOSS

111

Work Sheet & Trade Record

Contract Month & Year ———— Commodity ———— Page ————

DATE	HIGH	LOW	CLOSE	DPA	APO	ADAR	ARVF	PDR	PDVF	CVF	CF	TI	FOR (DATE)	EF	ADD OR SUB. TO TI	ORDER GO LONG OR SHORT	AT ⊳ MTN	TRADE ACTION & ACT. FILL	TRADE PROFIT OR LOSS

Work Sheet & Trade Record

Contract Month & Year ——————— Commodity ——————— Page ———

DATE	HIGH	LOW	CLOSE	DPA	ARO	ADAR	ARVF	POR	PDVF	CYF	CF	TI	POR (RATE)	EF	ADD OR SBL TO TI	ORDER GO LONG OR SHORT AT > MTN	TRADE ACTION & ACT FLL	TRADE PROFIT OR LOSS

Work Sheet & Trade Record

Contract Month & Year _____ Commodity _____ Page _____

DATE	HIGH	LOW	CLOSE	DPA	ARO	ADAR	ARYF	PDR	PDYF	CYF	CF	TI	FOR (DATE)	EF	ADD OR SUB. TO TI	ORDER GO LONG OR SHORT	AT ≥ MTN	TRADE ACTION & ACT FLL	TRADE PROFIT OR LOSS

Work Sheet & Trade Record

Contract Month & Year _____ Commodity _____ Page _____

DATE	HIGH	LOW	CLOSE	DPA	ARO	ADAR	ARYF	PDR	PDVF	CYF	CF	TI	FDR (DATE)	EF	ADD OR SUB. TO TI	ORDER GO LONG OR SHORT / AT >=MTN	TRADE ACTION & ACT FLL	TRADE PROFIT OR LOSS

Work Sheet & Trade Record

Contract Month & Year _____ Commodity _____ Page _____

DATE	HIGH	LOW	CLOSE	DPA	AJO	ADAR	ARVF	PDR	PDVF	CVF	CF	TI	FOR (DATE)	EF	ADD OR SUB. TO TI	ORDER GO LONG OR SHORT	AT > MTN	TRADE ACTION & ACT. FLL	TRADE PROFIT OR LOSS

Work Sheet & Trade Record

Contract Month & Year _____ Commodity _____ Page _____

DATE	HIGH	LOW	CLOSE	DPA	ARO	ADAR	ARVF	PDR	PDVF	CVF	CF	TI	FOR (DATE)	EF	ADD OR SUB. TO TI	ORDER GO LONG OR SHORT AT ▷ MTN	TRADE ACTION & ACT. FILL	TRADE PROFIT OR LOSS